Test Yourself

Introduction to Psychology

Deborah R. Winters, Ph.D.
Department of Psychology
New Mexico State University
Las Cruces, NM

Contributing Editors

Patricia A. Crowe, M.A.
Department of Psychology
University of Northern Iowa
Cedar Falls, IA

Susanna M. Perry, Ph.D.
Department of Psychology and Sociology
Texas A&M International University
Laredo, TX

Katherine M. Demitrakis, Ph.D.
Department of Psychology
University of North Carolina–Asheville
Asheville, NC

D1604601

NTC LearningWorks
a division of *NTC Publishing Group*
Lincolnwood, Illinois

Library of Congress Cataloging-in-Publication Data
is available from the Library of Congress.

A *Test Yourself Books, Inc.* Project

Published by NTC Publishing Group
© 1996 NTC Publishing Group, 4255 West Touhy Avenue
Lincolnwood (Chicago), Illinois 60646-1975 U.S.A.

6 7 8 9 ML 0 9 8 7 6 5 4 3 2 1

Contents

Preface

Most likely, you purchased this book to help improve your test scores. One of the best ways to improve your scores in college is to improve your memory. Psychologists have identified several ways to do that. The study of memory is covered in the area of thinking, or cognitive psychology. Improving your memory can improve performance in all of your academic courses.

Another key element in the improvement of test scores is to get information about a subject area from multiple perspectives. Personally, I chose this as the topic for my doctoral research when in graduate school, and discovered that instead of rereading the same material multiple times, it is more beneficial to look at a subject from yet *another* perspective. The use of multiple perspectives results in a type of "deeper" knowledge.

There are a variety of ways in which you can gain multiple perspectives in a college course. For example, your instructor's lectures provide an additional perspective to that of the textbook. You could also read an *additional* textbook that is not required, but you might not have the spare time to do so.

Finally, yet another way to improve your scores is to test yourself, to determine where your weak areas are. Typically that happens when you receive your examination grade. However, this book will allow you to test your knowledge of a topic *before* you arrive at the exam in the classroom, affording you the opportunity to assess your knowledge ahead of time, while there is still the chance to take some action.

Deborah R. Winters, Ph.D.

How to Use this Book

This "Test Yourself" book is part of a unique series designed to help you improve your test scores on almost any type of examination you will face. Too often, you will study for a test—quiz, midterm, or final—and come away with a score that is lower than anticipated. Why? Because there is no way for you to really know how much you understand a topic until you've taken a test. The *purpose* of the test, after all, is to test your complete understanding of the material.

The "Test Yourself" series offers you a way to improve your scores and to actually test your knowledge at the time you use this book. Consider each chapter a diagnostic pretest in a specific topic. Answer the questions, check your answers, and then give yourself a grade. Then, and only then, will you know where your strengths and, more important, weaknesses are. Once these areas are identified, you can strategically focus your study on those topics that need additional work.

Each book in this series presents a specific subject in an organized manner, and although each "Test Yourself" chapter may not correspond to exactly the same chapter in your textbook, you should have little difficulty in locating the specific topic you are studying. Written by educators in the field, each book is designed to correspond, as much as possible, to the leading textbooks. This means that you can feel confident in using this book, and that regardless of your textbook, professor, or school, you will be much better prepared for anything you will encounter on your test.

Each chapter has four parts:

Brief Yourself. All chapters contain a brief overview of the topic that is intended to give you a more thorough understanding of the material with which you need to be familiar. Sometimes this information is presented at the beginning of the chapter, and sometimes it flows throughout the chapter, to review your understanding of various *units* within the chapter.

Test Yourself. Each chapter covers a specific topic corresponding to one that you will find in your textbook. Answer the questions, either on a separate page or directly in the book, if there is room.

Check Yourself. Check your answers. Every question is fully answered and explained. These answers will be the key to your increased understanding. If you answered the question incorrectly, read the explanations to *learn* and *understand* the material. You will note that at the end of every answer you will be referred to a specific subtopic within that chapter, so you can focus your studying and prepare more efficiently.

Grade Yourself. At the end of each chapter is a self-diagnostic key. By indicating on this form the numbers of those questions you answered incorrectly, you will have a clear picture of your weak areas.

There are no secrets to test success. Only good preparation can guarantee higher grades. By utilizing this "Test Yourself" book, you will have a better chance of improving your scores and understanding the subject more fully.

What Is Psychology About?

1

Brief Yourself

As a field, psychology is the study of behavior and mental processes. It shares the same basic goals of research in any science: to describe, understand, predict, and control (or influence). Clinical psychology is what most people think of when they hear the term "psychology." It is concerned with the assessment and treatment of people suffering from a psychological malady. Most topics in the field can be viewed from several perspectives, and each sheds light on our understanding of human behavior. For example, some perspectives include biology/evolution, learning/behaviorist, cognitive/information processing, psychodynamic/humanist, and sociocultural. Each perspective offers a different set of causal factors underlying behavior and each contributes to both the scientific goals and the therapeutic applications.

Test Yourself

1. What is the scientific attitude?

2. What is the scientific method?

3. What is the difference between basic and applied research?

4. What is the difference between descriptive and experimental research?

5. Give a brief example of how several of the perspectives contribute to psychology as a science.

6. Give a brief example of how several of the perspectives contribute to clinical psychology and possible therapeutic applications.

7. What is the difference between a clinical psychologist and a psychiatrist?

8. What is the "nature-nurture" controversy?

9. Can behavior be explained in terms of either nature or nurture?

10. Some people believe psychology is merely common sense. Is it? Explain.

11. What is the difference between a dependent and an independent variable?

12. Why is the scientific attitude especially important when seeking answers to psychological questions?

13. As a research tool, can correlational studies show cause-effect relationships?

14. Why are statistics important when studying psychology?

15. What is the difference between "psychologizing" and psychology?

16. If I study psychology, will I be able to control what other people do and what other people think?

17. If I study psychology, will I be able to control my own thinking?

18. How might a small-business owner use psychological principles in managing her employees?

19. Can psychology help to understand how children learn?

20. Give an example of how psychology might help you understand something your parents or grandparents might do, such as not understanding what you say.

21. What kind of careers are available in psychology?

Check Yourself

1. The scientific attitude describes an approach to answering questions. Scientists persistently ask "What do you mean?" and "How do you know?" In this sense a scientist is skeptical. Scientists also let the evidence lead to the conclusions, not the other way around; science is not looking for evidence to confirm our beliefs while ignoring that which contradicts it. This means some answers to questions are not in the realm of science, such as believing in life after death or the existence of a supreme being; holding these beliefs requires an act of faith. Acts of faith are not open to scientific scrutiny because the "how" cannot be tested, confirmed, or falsified. **(Science)**

2. The scientific method describes a means of testing evidence and explaining phenomena. It begins with a theory, an interrelated set of ideas used to explain the phenomenon of interest. A hypothesis is a specific, testable proposition that derives from the theory, which leads to a specific prediction or outcome if the theory is correct. The scientist next collects data relevant to the prediction, analyzes it, and compares the results with the prediction. If the two are in accord, the theory is upheld; if not, the scientist must find out why. The results are then used to modify, expand, or revise the theory, new testable hypotheses are developed, data is collected and analyzed, and so on. This continuous interplay and refinement of understanding is the scientific method. **(Science)**

3. Basic research is the quest for knowledge for its own sake, to discover the basic facts about a phenomenon. Applied research is aimed to solve a particular problem. For example, discovering whether short-term memory has a capacity limit and what it might be is a basic research issue; designing an airplane cockpit warning system so short-term memory is not overloaded with too many things at once is an applied research problem. **(Research)**

4. Descriptive research describes the phenomenon of interest without attempting to explain how or why it came to be. Most assessment tests in clinical applications are descriptive and it remains for the therapist to determine *why* a problem exists and how to treat it. Experimental research attempts to answer the *how* and *why* questions. It does this by manipulating one or a few variables in a controlled setting, holding everything else constant, and observing the results as the variables change. This leads to the other primary distinction between the two types of research. Experimental research can provide a causal mechanism for a phenomenon, but descriptive research cannot. Descriptive research is limited to identifying when traits or phenomena might co-occur, but it cannot say why. **(Research)**

5. From the biological perspective it has been discovered that there are particular brain structures or neural pathways and certain behaviors are associated with them; for example, some types of epileptic seizures are eliminated by lesioning a small area of the brain. From the learning perspective, classical conditioning, operant conditioning, and modeling all demonstrate the associative nature of human learning and what the requirements are for an association to be formed. From a social psychological perspective, the James-Lange theory of emotion, is that if we deliberately act in a way different from the way we feel, we can change our "thinking"; for example, if we feel sad, but force ourselves to greet people with a smile, walk with a bounce in our step, and so on, in a short while we will notice that we don't feel sad anymore and that our mood is improved. **(What is psychology?4)**

6. The discovery of neurotransmitters as the basis of neural communication has led to major strides in drug therapy for maladies such as depression or Parkinson's disease. Phobias are often treated with systematic desensitization, a classical conditioning procedure. Cognitive therapies view maladaptive behaviors as due to faulty thinking patterns, so therapy from this perspective emphasizes changing logical errors in thinking. As the faulty thinking is corrected, the maladaptive behavior is replaced by a healthy one. **(Applications of psychology)**

7. A clinical psychologist has completed his undergraduate work and earned a doctorate in psychology. The work involves training in research, clinical skills, and an internship. A psychiatrist is a medical doctor who performs several years of residency training in psychiatry after medical school. Because of the medical training, psychiatrists are permitted to prescribe drugs, electroshock treatment, and other biological interventions, but psychologists are not. **(Psychology vs. psychiatry)**

8. The nature-nurture controversy concerns the relative importance of biological (genetic/heredity) and experiential (environmental/learning) factors in behavior. For example, the current view is that intelligence is due both to a genetic endowment and how much that endowment is actualized or stimulated (i.e., proper nutrition for growth, stimulating environment, and so on). The nature-nurture controversy is false in that both interact. **(Understanding behavior)**

9. No. The so-called nature-nurture controversy is a false dichotomy because you cannot have one without the other. For example, plant two genetically identical seeds, give them each a different amount of water, and they will grow to different heights. Conversely, plant two genetically different seeds and give them identical amounts of water, fertilizer, and the like, and they will grow to different heights. In the first example, the variation in height attained by the identical seeds can be attributed to environmental (nurture) causes. In the second example the variation in height is due to biological (nature) factors. Both the seed along with the water and fertilizer are necessary for a plant to grow; take away the seed (nature) or the nutrients (nurture), and there will be no plant. This is just as true for our plant as it is for more complex life-forms such as human beings. **(Understanding behavior)**

10. No, psychology is not merely common sense. Common sense and intuition are types of subconscious "reasoning"; they are often effective for simple, concrete-bound connections (such as why a square peg will not fit into a round hole), but are prone to error for anything more complex. For example, our common sense and intuition both tell us that for romantic attraction, absence makes the heart grow fonder. Yet we know just as strongly that out-of-sight is out-of-mind. Psychology can explain this seeming contradiction; common sense and intuition cannot. **(What is psychology)**

11. An independent variable is some factor or aspect of a situation that the experiment manipulates (changes). In contract, a dependent variable is the response of the person or animal, as a result of being exposed to the dependent variable. **(Research)**

12. With the so-called "hard" sciences such as chemistry or structural engineering, all of the factors affecting a particular outcome can be controlled once they are identified; this allows for straightforward testing of cause-effect relationships. This is not true in psychology. Even though we may suspect a particular relationship—say, between parenting styles and a child's self-esteem—ethical considerations do not allow us to force other parents and their children to behave in a particular way so as to test our hypothesis. So the difficulty of establishing the "how do you know" is much more difficult in psychology than in some other fields. Also, psychology is much more personal than, say, structural engineering: If, for example, it is discovered that a particular type of building foundation does not stand up well to earthquakes, only people who are concerned about this type of structural stress will do anything different. On the other hand, if you claim that self-esteem must be based on actual accomplishment and not just positive verbal feedback, you may well have to argue against the beliefs of many parents and policies of school systems. Not only are the issues psychology deals with more complex, but the "how do you know" is often equally complicated. **(Research)**

13. What determines whether research can show a cause-effect relationship is the experimental design and the testing of a causal mechanism. This is true in any field, not just psychology. Most research in psychology is correlational; using an experimental design, the researcher can argue for a cause-effect relationship. A correlation, the co-occurrence of two phenomena, does not satisfy this requirement; for example, hair

length and gender are highly correlated in many cultures, yet no one would argue that gender causes hair to grow to a predetermined length. (**Research**)

14. Statistics are important when studying psychology for three main reasons. First, they give a researcher the means to describe and quantify phenomena in objective terms. Second, inferential statistics provides a researcher with a method to evaluate the phenomena. Third, objective descriptions and measurements can be communicated to others with (comparatively) little misunderstanding allowing the work to be replicated. Statistics are not a substitute for good thinking or sound experimental design; they are only a tool to help us in our quest for new understanding. (**Statistics**)

15. "Psychologizing" is judging someone in terms of the motives attributed to him instead of by his behavior. A person is psychologizing when he condemns someone who achieves a great accomplishment, but does so for the wrong reasons, at least according to the psychologizer. (For example, the owner of a successful business is condemned if she started it because she wanted to make money — making money is considered "bad" in the eyes of the psychologizer.) The reverse is also true, that heinous acts are excused because the motives were good. In psychology the focus is on observable behavior because this can be known with certainty, whereas internal motives that exist in the mind of the actor cannot be seen by anyone but him. (**How psychology is used**)

16. No, psychology will not enable you to control what other people do or what other people think. Brainwashing has been shown to have limited effect in altering people's thinking, and it is primarily effective when they are physically restrained, such as in a POW camp. There is no way known to "force" someone to truly change his thinking; he can act differently, and say things to make you believe he has changed his mind, but there is no way to tell if he has indeed changed or is just putting on a show. (**How psychology is used**)

17. By studying psychology you will gain insight into your thinking, gain a better understanding of things that affect cognition. You may become more attuned to your own emotions and discover how other people's moods can affect you. Clarity of thought and increased awareness of how internal and external forces affect you, is the type of "control" you attain over your thinking. (**How psychology is used**)

18. If she wants to increase the employees' commitment to the company so they are less likely to take jobs with a competitor, is higher salary the best solution, or should she look at other issues such as group dynamics (co-worker relationships), sense of responsibility, ability of employees to control their own work/outcome, feelings of boredom or excitement, feelings of job security/insecurity, and so on? Psychology can help her answer these kinds of questions. (**Applications of psychology**)

19. Jean Piaget is the father of developmental psychology. He discovered that children learn things in a predictable sequence, and that until a child has mastered more elementary principles, he cannot learn more sophisticated ones. Prior to Piaget's work, children were viewed as miniature adults. He questioned this, and through a lifetime's work he devised tasks and mapped out how children learn. Those who followed Piaget have expanded on his work and continue to do so, but it was Piaget who discovered that infants and children learn differently than do mature adults. (**Psychology and children**)

20. One of your parents or grandparents complains that he cannot understand people in conversation anymore. You suggest that his sense of hearing is declining and that he get a hearing aid. He does, but he still can't understand people when they are talking to him. The real reason may not be a decline in hearing, but a reduced short-term memory capacity (one of the effects of aging). You can test this by speaking a little bit slower (instead of louder) while talking with him. By speaking slower, you don't overload his reduced STM. If he looks at your face when you are talking, that might help, too. (**Applications of psychology**)

21. Slightly more than half the members of the American Psychological Association have careers in which they engage in therapy. Educational and school psychologists study issues related to learning and teaching, sometimes in a school setting, other times at a college for training and research. Businesses employ human-factors psychologists to help design better human-machine interfaces, and industrial and organizational psychologists to evaluate business organizations, employee behavior, and the like. Research specialties, such as in a university setting, include personality psychologists, social psychologists, and experimental psychologists, to name a few. **(Careers in psychology)**

Grade Yourself

Circle the numbers of the questions you missed, then fill in the total incorrect for each topic. If you answered more than three questions incorrectly, you need to focus on that topic. (If a topic has less than three questions and you had at least one wrong, we suggest you study that topic also. Read your textbook, a review book, or ask your teacher for help.)

Subject: What is Psychology About?

Topic	Question Numbers	Number Incorrect
Scientific attitude	1	
Scientific method	2	
Research	3, 4	
What is psychology?	5, 10	
Applications of psychology	6, 18, 20	
Psychology vs. psychiatry	7	
Understanding behavior	8, 9	
Research	11, 12, 13	
Statistics	14	
How psychology is used	15, 16, 17	
Psychology and children	19	
Careers in psychology	21	

Infancy and Childhood

2

Brief Yourself

Developmental psychology includes the study of the life cycle, starting with conception and progressing to the point of death. The period of infancy involves rapid changes during the time in the womb. After birth, babies grow quickly. As the senses of the infant develop, it is able to learn more effectively about the environment. The psychology of childhood includes the examination of how children develop in a physical, social, and cognitive way.

Test Yourself

1. Discuss the three major philosophical debates in the history of developmental psychology.

2. Describe the cross-sectional method for studying development, as compared to the longitudinal method.

3. What are genes? How are they important to human development?

4. How are the X and Y chromosomes different? What roles do they play?

5. Describe the role of testosterone in the unborn child.

6. How are identical twins different from fraternal twins?

7. How does conception occur? What is a risk involved during the day or two afterward?

8. Provide a brief description of each of the three stages of prenatal development.

9. What are teratogens? Give some examples.

10. What causes fetal alcohol syndrome? How does it affect a newborn?

11. What reflexes can be found in a newborn? Why are reflexes important to the newborn?

12. Define habituation. Explain how habituation is important to research on perception in the newborn.

13. Explain the process of visual development in the newborn.

14. What are the developmental changes seen in auditory development?

15. How does brain development progress in infancy?

16. What is brain plasticity? Why is it important?

17. Define cognition.

18. How are assimilation and accommodation different?

19. What is the first stage in Piaget's theory of cognitive development? Describe it.

20. What is the second stage in Piaget's theory of cognitive development? Describe it.

21. What is the third stage in Piaget's theory of cognitive development? Describe it.

22. What is the fourth stage in Piaget's theory of cognitive development? Describe it.

23. What is object permanence? Give an explanation.

24. What are some current views of Piaget's theory of cognitive development?

25. Define egocentrism in the child.

26. What is stranger anxiety?

27. Define attachment.

28. Compare attachment to imprinting.

29. Discuss the research on attachment and specify the types of attachment that have been identified.

30. When does the self-concept develop? How can it be identified in a child?

31. Discuss fathering versus mothering. Explain the typical relationships between fathers and their infants.

32. Mention four styles of parenting, in addition to providing pros and cons of each style.

33. What is temperament?

Check Yourself

1. Three key issues that have been debated for years by psychologists and philosophers are those of: (a) nature versus nurture; (b) continuity versus stages; and (c) stability versus change. Nature refers to the influence of inborn, biological aspects, such as genetics, on development, whereas nurture refers to the environment or experiences a person gains over time. The consensus is now that nature and nurture interact and both play important roles. In the continuity-versus-stages debate, continuity refers to a gradual, continuous progression of developmental change, whereas according to the stage view, development makes noticeable leaps and proceeds through a series of separate steps. Some researchers emphasize continuity in the development of theories and research, whereas others emphasize the stage idea. Finally, stability refers to personality traits that are present at birth and tend to remain present throughout the lifespan. In contrast, change addresses what does not remain constant in the person. Most developmental psychologists now have evidence that there is continuity over the lifespan for certain traits, such as temperament. (**History**)

2. The cross-sectional method allows researchers to observe or test people of various ages at approximately the same point in time. By comparing the responses of people in more than one age group, the psychologist can determine whether there are differences in behavior at different ages. Using the longitudinal method, the same group is studied repeatedly over some period of time, such as over the span of a month, year, or several years. (**Research methods**)

3. Genes are biochemical components of heredity. They are found strung along the DNA molecules that form double helix structures in the chromosomes. The chromosomes are threadlike structures found in each cell in the human body. In fact, each cell contains twenty-three pairs of chromosomes. Genes are important, because they carry information about eye color, body size, personality, etc., to be carried from generation to generation. Genes also transmit general information about being human, such as standing upright, having two hands and feet, having thumbs, and so on. (**Heredity**)

4. Both males and females have an X chromosome as one-half of the twenty-third pair. The egg always provides an X chromosome. However, some sperm carry an X chromosome and some carry a Y chromosome. Depending on the particular sperm that reaches and fertilizes the egg, the fertilized egg will contain either an XX pair or an XY pair. If the twenty-third pair is XX, the fertilized egg will develop into a female. If it is XY, it will develop into a male. Therefore, it is the father, rather than the mother, who determines the sex of the offspring. (**Heredity**)

5. Of all the masculinizing hormones, testosterone is the most important. Testosterone stimulates growth of the male sex organs while in the fetus. It is also crucial in the masculinization of the boy at the time of puberty, including the development of pubic hair, facial and underarm hair, the deepening of the voice, and the enlargement of the penis and testicles. Testosterone is also found in females, but in much smaller amounts. (**Hormones**)

6. Identical twins develop from one fertilized egg that splits in half as it moves down the fallopian tube. Each half then remains separate and develops on its own, such that two embryos result, each with identical genetic information. In contrast, fraternal twins develop from two separate eggs. Rarely, two eggs will be released by a female at the time of ovulation. If so, the two eggs are generally released within twenty-four hours of each other. In the case of fraternal twins, two different sperm fertilize the two eggs, resulting in two embryos, each of which has completely unique genetic information. (**Genetics**)

7. Conception refers to the moment that the sperm from the father unites with the egg of the mother and fertilizes it. Fertilization typically takes place in the outer one-third of the fallopian tube. The term for the

one-celled organism that consists of the united sperm and egg is a "zygote." As the fertilized egg moves down the fallopian tube to the womb, or uterus, it continues to divide and differentiate, forming a multi-celled organism that must then burrow into the lining of the uterus, which is a risky process, in that only about half of all fertilized eggs successfully embed themselves into the uterine lining. **(Prenatal development)**

8. The three stages of prenatal development consist of: (a) the period of the zygote (conception to two weeks); (b) the period of the embryo (two weeks through eight weeks); and (c) the period of the fetus (nine weeks through birth). Another way to look at prenatal development is to divide it into three equal trimesters. **(Prenatal development)**

9. Teratogens are harmful substances that can cross through the barrier of the placenta and potentially injure the developing embryo and fetus. Teratogens include a wide variety of substances such as alcohol; nicotine; legal drugs, such as aspirin and Accutane (acne medication); illegal drugs, such as cocaine and heroin; viruses, such as rubella, AIDS, and herpes; bacteria, such as gonorrhea and syphilis; and even pollutants, such as carbon monoxide, lead, and mercury. Teratogens were discovered in the 1920s, when a physician realized that if a pregnant woman contracted rubella (German measles) during the first trimester, the developing child was likely to be affected by characteristic deformities. **(Risks in prenatal development)**

10. Fetal alcohol syndrome, or FAS, is typically seen when a pregnant woman drinks excessive amounts of alcohol. At present, researchers are unsure of to how much alcohol constitutes too much. Therefore, it is recommended that pregnant women consume no alcohol. Alcohol in a pregnant woman's bloodstream crosses over to her fetus and decreases activity in its developing central nervous system, putting it at risk for lifelong brain abnormalities. FAS babies also typically have small, misproportioned heads. **(Risks in prenatal development)**

11. Babies are born with a limited set of reflex behaviors, allowing them to have better chances of survival. Reflexes, in that they are present from birth, do not have to be learned. Some reflexes of the newborn include sucking, breathing, rooting (turning the head to suck on whatever touches the cheek), swallowing, blinking, the Moro reflex (throwing the arms up and out as the result of a loud noise, or having support taken out from underneath), and the Babinski reflex (curling the toes up and out in a fanning motion as a result of having the bottom of the feet stroked). A reflex, such as sucking, allows the infant to get nourishment more successfully. Most reflexes at birth are related to basic survival, whereas others, such as the Moro and Babinski reflexes, are informative as to the maturation of the brain. Such reflexes are often not present in preterm babies. **(Newborn behavior)**

12. Habituation is a form of learning that is very basic. During habituation, the infant becomes less and less attentive to incoming stimuli that are repeatedly put before him or her. Using habituation, developmental psychologists are able to discover what the infant is paying attention to and what he prefers to pay attention to, without having to rely on words, in that the infant cannot speak. Habituation has enabled professionals in the discovery that infants as young as seven hours old can tell the difference between certain colors, shapes, and sounds. **(Newborn behavior)**

13. Infants are born nearsighted, so objects must be close enough for the newborn to see them clearly. Newborns tend to prefer complex rather than simple stimuli, and prefer looking at human faces versus nonhuman visual patterns or color samples. Gazing at faces seems to facilitate in the development of social interaction. Depth perception seems to exist even in infants who are not old enough to crawl. However, actual fear of heights develops only after infants begin to crawl and move about. **(Perception)**

14. Young infants hear remarkably well, and within minutes of being born, newborns will turn their heads in the direction of loud noises. Newborns as young as three weeks old have shown they can tell the difference between the voice of their mother and the voice of a woman who is a stranger. (**Perception**)

15. When an infant is born, it has about all the brain cells it ever will have. Throughout life, brain cells die, but they do not regenerate. How the infant learns is through the growth of neural connections between the existing brain cells. Sensory and physical stimulation serve to encourage the development of neural connections in the brain. Preterm babies who receive plenty of physical stimulation have been shown to develop faster neurologically than those who do not. (**Physical development**)

16. Brain plasticity means that if part of the brain is damaged, other areas sometimes reorganize and assume the functions of the damaged area. In the brains of young children, brain functions have not become rigidly designated, so there is a great deal more plasticity than in the brain of an adult. (**Physical development**)

17. Cognition refers to mental capabilities, such as memory, language, reasoning, and problem solving, that are associated with thinking. (**Cognitive development**)

18. Assimilation occurs when there is interpretation of new information, which roughly fits into existing cognitive schemas, or frameworks of understanding. Assimilation is sorting information into an existing schema. In contrast, accommodation occurs when existing cognitive schemas become revised. An example of accommodation would be when the child realizes that the "kitty" schema is too broad and accommodates by refinement of the category, so that it no longer includes lions and tigers. (**Cognitive development**)

19. Sensorimotor: birth to age two. Infants begin to separate the self from others, explore the physical properties of objects, learn that objects exist even when not in view (object permanence), imitate others, speak and understand simple words. (**Cognitive development**)

20. Preoperational: two to seven. Language develops rapidly but is often used egocentrically. Cognition is limited. (**Cognitive development**)

21. Concrete operational: seven to eleven. Cognition becomes logical and more adultlike. The child reasons about the quality of objects and comes to understand conversation. (**Cognitive development**)

22. Formal operational: twelve to adult. The person exhibits flexible cognition, abstract reasoning, and learns to form and evaluate hypotheses. (**Cognitive development**)

23. Object permanence is the notion that an object continues to exist even after it disappears from view. Infants between eight to eleven months of age can search for and retrieve an object hidden in a single location, which demonstrates the idea of object permanence. Before that age, infants behave as though an object that is out of sight is also "out of mind." (**Cognitive development**)

24. Historically, Piaget's work is very important. Today, some psychologists question Piaget, and wonder if children's cognitive abilities really do progress in abrupt stages, given that there is more evidence for continuity. Also, object permanence might develop earlier than Piaget originally thought. However, most psychologists agree with Piaget as to the idea that children actively create an understanding of the world in a way that is unique and different from the way that adults think. (**Piagetian theory**)

25. Egocentrism means that the child is unable to view the world from another person's perspective. In other words, he or she cannot imagine what others experience. Egocentrism does not refer to selfish behavior. (**Social development**)

26. Stranger anxiety refers to a fear of unknown people. It typically begins during the sensorimotor stage, at about eight months of age—the same time that an understanding of object permanence occurs. It is a normal phenomenon that children grow out of, but when a child experiences it, there can be crying and fear when a child realizes he or she will be left with a baby-sitter, for example. (**Social development**)

27. Attachment is a strong connection between the infant and the primary caregivers. It is a bond that is a basic form of love. Ainsworth studied attachment and found that some children develop secure attachment. Secure attachment is a positive characteristic that allows them to seek out contact with the caregiver. In contrast, some children develop various forms of insecure attachment, in which they are too dependent on the caregiver, for example. (**Social development**)

28. Infants stay close to people with whom they have formed an attachment and will explore unfamiliar places and objects in the presence of that person. If they are separated from the person they are attached to, they will cry or fuss. Infants help draw their parents into a close relationship through rewarding behaviors, such as smiling, gazing, and vocalizing, bringing parents and infants together. Attachment can be strengthened through touch, as discovered by Harlow. It used to be thought that feeding activity strengthened attachment, but it is now known that touch is even more important than food in forming the basic bond of attachment. In contrast, Lorenz examined the more rigid attachment process, called "imprinting,"which is found in waterbirds and occurs immediately after birth, during a limited, critical period. Surprisingly, Lorenz discovered that ducklings would follow the first person, animal, or object seen after birth. (**Social development**)

29. Ainsworth identified a difference between secure and insecure attachment. According to her studies, secure attachment is positive and desirable. Securely attached children come to act as leaders in school and are confident to explore the world. On the other hand, insecurely attached children can be either overdependent on a parent or remain somewhat aloof. (**Social development**)

30. The self-concept develops gradually over the first year. It can be identified in a child by observing to see if he or she notices his or her own reflection in a mirror. Most children have a self-concept by the time they are fifteen to eighteen months old. (**Social development**)

31. Of course, fathers like to hold, touch, and caress their infants, just as much as mothers do, but fathers are more likely to play physical games with infants, rather than to engage in traditional caregiving activities, such as bathing or feeding. Mothers are most likely to stimulate infants verbally by talking or reading to them. (**Parenting**)

32. Four main parenting styles include the permissive, authoritarian, authoritative, and rejecting/neglecting parent. Typically, a permissive parent, in which he or she makes few demands of the child and goes along with the child's wishes excessively, neglects to provide rules, making it difficult for the child to follow rules at school or in society. The authoritarian, very strict style is also detrimental, in that it can lead to negative emotional responses in the child, such as fear of the parent and authority figures, lying behavior, and low self-esteem. The most desirable parenting style is the authoritative, or democratic, style, in which the child is allowed to express preferences. There are still rules, but the parent explains the rules, follows through when they are broken, and modifies rules when necessary. The authoritative style typically leads to the most well adjusted people in adulthood. In contract, a rejecting/neglecting parent avoids the child and/or is not successful in providing basic needs, such as a safe environment, nutritious foods, or adequate time for interaction. (**Parenting**)

33. Temperament includes basic, inborn characteristics of personality, such as emotional excitability. Some children have been found to be more easy-going and cheerful as infants, whereas others are more irritable, and unpredictable when it comes to sleeping and eating patterns. (**Social development**)

Grade Yourself

Circle the numbers of the questions you missed, then fill in the total incorrect for each topic. If you answered more than three questions incorrectly, you need to focus on that topic. (If a topic has less than three questions and you had at least one wrong, we suggest you study that topic also. Read your textbook, a review book, or ask your teacher for help.)

Subject: Infancy and Childhood

Topic	Question Numbers	Number Incorrect
History	1	
Research methods	2	
Heredity	3, 4	
Hormones	5	
Genetics	6	
Prenatal development	7, 8	
Risks in prenatal development	9, 10	
Newborn behavior	11, 12	
Perception	13, 14	
Physical development	15, 16	
Cognitive development	17, 18, 19, 20, 21, 22, 23	
Piagetian theory	24	
Social development	25, 26, 27, 28, 29, 30, 33	
Parenting	31, 32	

Adolescence and Adulthood

3

Brief Yourself

Today, psychologists consider human development to be a lifelong process. Development during adolescence and adulthood, like childhood, can be examined in terms of physical, cognitive, and social change. Adolescence, beginning with puberty and ending with independence from the parent, is the transitional time period between childhood and adulthood. In comparison, adulthood is commonly broken down into the three time periods of early, middle, and late adulthood. As people age, the influence of experience causes the course of development to widen, with less of an ability to predict how a person will be. Despite wide individual differences in adulthood, there is still a number of commonalities people share. The proportion of elderly Americans is growing and is estimated to continue growing into the twenty-first century.

Test Yourself

1. Describe some general, physical changes that occur at about the time of puberty.

2. Name Piaget's stage of cognitive development that coincides with the onset of adolescence. Specify what happens during this stage.

3. Give details about Kohlberg's theory of moral reasoning.

4. Critique Kohlberg's theory of moral reasoning.

5. How does Erikson describe the time of adolescence?

6. What are four problems that can occur as part of the adolescent's search for identity?

7. According to Erikson, what is the major social task of young adulthood?

8. What does research show about the so-called "generation gap"?

9. How are primary sex characteristics different from secondary ones?

10. What is menarche? Mention what causes it.

11. How have sexually transmitted diseases, such as AIDS, changed the sexual practice of teens?

12. Why aren't teenagers in the United States likely to use birth control?

13. Why are teenage pregnancies so high in the United States, compared to other Western nations? What factors are involved?

14. What risks, in addition to teen pregnancy, are adolescents especially susceptible to?

15. What is a social clock?

16. What are the key physical changes that occur in middle adulthood?

17. Discuss the effects of age on sexuality. What happens for men? What happens for women?

18. What is the main cognitive change that takes place in middle adulthood?

19. What is Levinson's stage theory of adult social development about? Why is Levinson's theory controversial?

20. Describe the work that is being done to define and understand male menopause.

21. What are the key social changes that take place in adulthood, according to Erikson?

22. Discuss marital satisfaction during the period of early and middle adulthood.

23. What are some of the ways that divorce affects men and women and their children

24. What are the key physical changes that occur in later life?

25. What physiological conditions cause the end of menstruation?

26. Describe the physical symptoms often associated with female menopause.

27. How might people think differently as they age? Discuss cognitive changes in the elderly.

28. What is Alzheimer's disease?

29. What stages did Elisabeth Kübler-Ross discover that a person tends to experience upon learning of a terminal illness? List the stages in the correct order and discuss each one.

30. What types of social support systems are available for dying people?

increased in the last decade. Teenagers today are more likely to be at risk because of exposure to a variety of illegal drugs, compared to teenagers prior to the 1960s. **(Social issues in adolescence)**

15. A social clock refers to the information and encouragement one gets from friends, relatives, and society, as to the appropriate time to engage in activities such as graduation from college, getting married, buying a home, having a child, getting a job, etc. If a person chooses to live life in a way that does not match social expectations, he or she might find it frustrating to endure constant "reminders" from people, such as "When are you going to find the right guy? You don't want to be an old maid, do you? Would you like me to arrange a date for you with my co-worker's son?" Social clocks differ from society to society. They also change over time within a given society. **(Social issues in adolescence)**

16. There is a slow decline of the body's physical capabilities during middle adulthood. The capacity of the lungs declines, as does the pumping capacity of the heart. Energy expended at rest declines, and so does maximum energy expended when the body performs physical labor. Muscular strength and reaction also peak at the mid-twenties and start to decline thereafter. Hearing loss occurs, more so for men than for women. All of the senses become less sensitive throughout the twenties and beyond. **(Physical development in adulthood)**

17. As both men and women age, the reproductive system changes. In middle adulthood, men typically need more time to attain an erection and also need more time between ejaculation and the next penile erection. Men also experience a decline in sperm count as they age. Most men experience a sexual "prime" in the twenties, whereas women tend to reach their prime in the decade of the thirties. Women tend to experience greater ability to attain orgasm in middle adulthood, perhaps due to less anxiety over getting pregnant, or due to better knowledge of how their bodies function. It might also be due to the fact that the children have grown up and there is more marital privacy and perhaps they have more time to devote to sex. In middle age, there is some shrinkage in the size of the reproductive organs in females. Women tend to see more age-related effects on sexual physiology after the time of menopause than before. **(Physical development in adulthood)**

18. A key cognitive change during adulthood is that of a decline in recall memory. There are wide individual differences in cognitive ability among adults, making it difficult to identify general changes, but typically, recall memory suffers, whereas recognition memory does not. Studies conducted in a longitudinal manner have shown that fluid intelligence decreases with age, whereas crystallized intelligence increases. (Fluid and crystallized intelligence are defined in answer 27.) **(Cognitive development in adulthood)**

19. Levinson described a series of stages alternating with periods of change that adults progress through. Recent research has found that periods of crisis or change fluctuate widely from person to person, rather than at specific ages, as Levinson originally thought. **(Social development in adulthood)**

20. As a result of Levinson's interviews with middle-aged men, he described a form of "male menopause" or mid-life crisis, in which men are more likely to make radical life changes, involving a job or a marriage. Today, the idea of a male menopause is under debate by psychologists. **(Social development in adulthood)**

21. The development of intimacy, including the task of forming close relationships, primarily occurs early in adulthood, whereas in middle adulthood the main social task includes the need to feel productive. Erikson called this "generativity." **(Social development in adulthood)**

22. The divorce rate has risen over the past two decades. However, married men and women tend to report feeling happier than single, divorced, or widowed people. Marital satisfaction tends to dip over the course of a marriage, perhaps due to boredom or due to the emotional energy, money, and increased time necessary to devote to one's children that tends to take away from resources that could be devoted to one's

✓ Check Yourself

1. The time of life referred to as "adolescence" starts with puberty. Puberty lasts approximately two years and consists of rapid development that starts in girls at about age eleven and in boys at age thirteen. A physical growth spurt occurs. Also, the reproductive organs begin to mature, as well as nonreproductive traits, such as the appearance of pubic hair, the growth of breasts in females, and the deepening of the voice and growth of facial hair in males. First-time menstruation occurs in females, and first-time ejaculation occurs in males. **(Physical changes in adolescence)**

2. At about age eleven or twelve, adolescents become capable of what Piaget called "formal operational thought." The formal operational stage is characterized by abstract, logical thinking, along with the ability to consider hypothetical situations. This ability allows teens to solve problems more effectively and also to consider ethical dilemmas. **(Cognitive changes in adolescence)**

3. According to Kohlberg, moral reasoning is dependent upon the formal operational period of cognitive thought. Like Piaget, Kohlberg believed there was a relationship between cognition and moral judgment. Kohlberg believed people are capable of reasoning at preconventional, conventional, and postconventional levels. In order to test moral reasoning, Kohlberg gave children, teens, and adults moral dilemmas, for which there were no correct answers. He had people provide solutions to each dilemma, and then he proceeded to examine the reasons behind the answers people gave. For example, if a person were thinking at the preconventional level, he or she would obey rules primarily to avoid being punished or to gain specific rewards. In contrast, if a person were thinking at the conventional level, he or she would abide by laws because "the law is the law." However, at the highest, postconventional level, people show a deeper understanding and sometimes challenge laws for higher values, such as by refusing to fight in a war due to the belief that human life is sacred. **(Cognitive changes in adolescence)**

4. Some critics of Kohlberg's theory state that action, or what people really do, is a part of morality, in addition to what people *say* they will do. Critics also say that the postconventional level is evident primarily in educated, middle-class people in countries where individual values are emphasized. Other critics, such as Gilligan, say that Kohlberg's stages demonstrate a bias toward males, because for women, morality is more a matter of thinking about people and caring for people in a concrete sense, rather than considering justice in an abstract way. **(Cognitive changes in adolescence)**

5. In Erikson's theory, the main social goal of adolescence is the development of an identity. Adolescents spend time trying out different roles in different situations, as they experiment with the development of the self. In school situations, they might act one way, and at home, another. Gradually, in Western societies, adolescents become comfortable with, and act in accordance with, a single "self." **(Social changes in adolescence)**

6. Sometimes, parents, friends, or teachers can encourage the development of a self, such as when the teen is prematurely encouraged to take on the career path of a parent, without giving the child a chance to explore career possibilities on his or her own. This problem is called "foreclosure." Sometimes teens take on a negative identity, as shown by wearing unusual clothing, colorful hairstyles, and body mutilation (tattooing or piercing various parts of the body to insert rings), becoming the opposite of what parental figures value. Erikson called this an example of a "negative identity." Another problem that can ensue is that of postponing the development of an identity, which Erikson referred to as a "moratorium." A moratorium, such as during military service or further education, can serve positive purposes, allowing the teenager more time in developing an identity he or she is confident about. Yet another problem is that of identity diffusion, during which the teen does not form a well-defined self. **(Social changes in adolescence)**

7. Erikson said young adulthood was the time to develop the capacity for intimacy — the ability to form emotionally close relationships. According to Erikson's theory, once a person has formed an identity and has a clear sense of who he or she is, he or she can develop relationships as a family member, a friend, or a spouse, for example. **(Social changes in adulthood)**

8. In a study in which adolescents were asked to wear "beepers" and to report what emotion they were feeling when the beeper went off at random times throughout the day, it was discovered that most felt more open with friends than with family members. For most teens, however, disagreements with family members are fairly minor. In most families in the United States, the generation gap is actually small. A Gallup poll in 1988 found that only 5 percent of teenagers don't get along at all with parents. Instead, most adolescents said that they were happy with the way things were in the family, and it turned out that they held political and religious beliefs, and ideas about what is important in life, that were very similar to parental values. If a teen has positive relationships with parents, research has shown he or she tends to have more positive relations with peers, too. The relationship with the parent tends to support the relationship with the peer. **(Social changes in adolescence)**

9. Primary sex characteristics are the ones directly involved in reproduction. During adolescence, the primary sex characteristics, including the vagina and penis, grow and mature. Secondary sex characteristics are ones that differentiate males from females, but are not directly involved in reproduction. In males, the production of sperm, the deepened voice, and the appearance of pubic and facial hair are secondary sex characteristics. In females, secondary sex characteristics include the development of breasts, the widening of the hips, and the appearance of pubic hair. **(Physical changes in adolescence)**

10. Menarche is the first menstrual period in females. It occurs at about age eleven or twelve and is due to increased levels of estrogen in the teenager's body. At the time of menarche, ovulation, or the release of an egg from an ovary, may or may not occur. Although sometimes the female experiences several menstrual periods before an egg is released, counting on the lack of an egg is not a reliable method of birth control. **(Physical changes in adolescence)**

11. The incidence at which high school students reported having sex increased during the 1970s and 1980s. The rate decreased by the 1990s, and psychologists believe it is because of a greater awareness of AIDS and other sexually transmitted diseases among teenagers. The pattern of more males than females having sex during the teen years has continued throughout, however. **(Social issues in adolescence)**

12. Teenagers in the United States are not very likely to use birth control during sex for a variety of reasons, including: ignorance about fertility and methods of birth control, high sex guilt, lack of communication with parents and/or partners about sex, use of alcohol that impairs judgment and releases inhibitions, and lack of role models using birth control on television and in films. **(Social issues in adolescence)**

13. Of all Western nations, the incidence of teenage pregnancy is the highest in the United States. Researchers have found that the teenage pregnancy rate is approximately 1 million girls per year in the U.S., and that this is more than double what other Western nations experience. It is thought that the high rate of teenage pregnancy in the U.S. is not due to more acts of intercourse, as it is thought that the rate of intercourse is very similar among teens in Western nations. Instead, teens in the U.S. are much less likely to use birth control. **(Social issues in adolescence)**

14. Adolescents show few signs of practicing safe sex and as a result are at risk for numerous sexually transmitted diseases. Other risks for adolescents are problems associated with poverty or a lack of supervision. Adolescents are also more at risk for suicide, compared to other age groups, and teen suicide rates are increasing at an alarming rate. Teenagers, especially black males, are increasingly more likely to be injured or killed as a result of violence. Teen arrests for committing violent crimes have also greatly

spouse. When children become independent and leave home, marital happiness frequently increases. Most people who divorce opt to remarry at some point. **(Social development in adulthood)**

23. After a divorce, men tend to have more psychological problems, whereas women tend to have more monetary difficulties. When parents get divorced, children are more at risk if they are in a transitional period, such as starting kindergarten or beginning to enter puberty. In general, boys tend to have more difficulty adjusting to divorce than girls do. Boys typically become more rebellious, perhaps because they resent having the mother as the custodial parent, as so often happens, or perhaps because the mother has less time to devote to discipline. **(Social development in adulthood)**

24. In later life, all the physical changes that began in early and middle adulthood continue to progress at an accelerated pace. Brain cells tend to die more readily. There is an increased likelihood of broken bones in females, due to the high incidence of osteoporosis. **(Physical development in late adulthood)**

25. Menstruation ends during a time called the "climacteric," which consists of the years during which the female body adapts to declining amounts of estrogen. Menopause, or cessation of menstruation, occurs at approximately age fifty. **(Physical development in late adulthood)**

26. Due to decreased estrogen production, the skin of the female becomes more dry; additionally, there is a drying of the vaginal tissues. Decreased estrogen also can result in decreased amounts of calcium in the bones, along with hot flashes. Hot flashes are due to vasomotor instability, such that the woman feels warm and sweaty at unpredictable times, as the blood vessels go through an adaption phase and do not always respond accurately according to the environmental conditions. **(Physical development in late adulthood)**

27. Crystalized intelligence refers to knowledge that one has accumulated over the lifespan. Fluid intelligence refers to the ability to reason abstractly. Research has shown that crystalized intelligence increases throughout life, whereas fluid intelligence decreases. However, it should be noted that general intelligence scores tend to depend on the type of tasks that are utilized. The aging process slows neural reactions, and leads to a gradual, yet small, loss in the number of brain cells. In general, most elderly people do not become senile. If a person continues to think and solve problems, cognitive abilities are more likely to function well. **(Cognitive development in late adulthood)**

28. Some small percentage of the elderly is afflicted with Alzheimer's disease, in which there is a major decline in memory capabilities. **(Cognitive development in late adulthood)**

29. Denial, anger, bargaining, depression, and acceptance are the stages described by Kübler-Ross. During the anger stage, a person is upset about the fact that he or she dying. During bargaining, he tries to make deals with God or with health care practitioners, in order to live longer. During depression, he becomes more removed from people and is saddened. During acceptance, if this stage should occur, he tends to realize that death is inevitable and proceeds to make peace with the world, putting the household and monetary affairs in order. **(Death and dying)**

30. Organizations, such as hospices, can provide care for the terminally ill person, by making services available twenty-four hours per day, providing live-in care, and by helping to ease the pain of the surviving family members. **(Death and dying)**

Grade Yourself

Circle the numbers of the questions you missed, then fill in the total incorrect for each topic. If you answered more than three questions incorrectly, you need to focus on that topic. (If a topic has less than three questions and you had at least one wrong, we suggest you study that topic also. Read your textbook, a review book, or ask your teacher for help.)

Subject: Adolescence and Adulthood

Topic	Question Numbers	Number Incorrect
Physical changes in adolescence	1, 9, 10	
Cognitive changes in adolescence	2, 3, 4	
Social changes in adolescence	5, 6, 8	
Social issues in adolescence	11, 12, 13, 14, 15	
Social changes in adulthood	7	
Physical development in adulthood	16, 17	
Cognitive development in adulthood	18	
Social development in adulthood	19, 20, 21, 22, 23	
Physical development in late adulthood	24, 25, 26	
Cognitive development in late adulthood	27, 28	
Death and dying	29, 30	

Biological Psychology

4

Brief Yourself

Biological psychologists are also known as behavioral neuroscientists, physiological psychologists, and biopsychologists. Biological psychology is concerned with the functions of the nervous system, including the brain and spinal cord. As a discipline, biological psychology examines the complex connections between biology and behavior. A major part of biological psychology is the continuing study of the brain. The brain is composed of many parts. It controls and monitors an organism's behaviors. Under the control of the brain, the nervous system and endocrine system work to coordinate voluntary and involuntary behaviors in both humans and animals, assisting in communication with the world outside the body.

Test Yourself

1. What is the term used to describe the study of personality by means of examining the bumps on a person's skull? Who developed the technique, and for what purpose?

2. What is a neuron, and what are the components that compose one?

3. What is the central nervous system?

4. What is the peripheral nervous system composed of?

5. What are the divisions of the autonomic nervous system, and what do they do?

6. What is an action potential, and how is one produced?

7. Describe the process by means of which nerve cells communicate.

8. Describe the simplest nerve pathway. Why is such a pathway important? Give an example.

9. What are neurotransmitters, and how do they work?

10. Name two types of neurotransmitters and describe their functions.

11. What are sensory neurons?

12. What are motor neurons?

13. What is the endocrine system?

14. What is the pituitary gland?

15. Give examples of techniques by which the brain can be scientifically examined.

16. What is the brain stem?

17. What are the various structures within the brain stem?

18. Describe the functions of the medulla.

19. Describe the functions of the reticular formation.

20. Describe the functions of the thalamus.

21. Describe the functions of the cerebellum.

22. What are the functions of the structures that make up the limbic system?

23. Describe the functions of the amygdala.

24. Describe the functions of the hypothalamus.

25. What is the portion of the brain that is called the "cerebral cortex"?

26. What are the locations and functions of each of the four lobes of the cerebral cortex?

27. Who is Phineas Gage, and why is he important in the understanding of the cortex?

28. What is the motor cortex, and what are its functions?

29. What is the sensory cortex, and what are its functions?

30. What parts of the cortex are most responsible for language processing? Where are they located? How can damage to different cortical areas impair language functioning?

31. How does handedness affect the processing of speech?

32. What is a split brain? Describe the research on the split brain. What does the research reveal?

Check Yourself

1. Franz Gall, a German physician, invented phrenology as a way to discover the mental abilities and personality characteristics of people, through scrutinizing the bumps and irregularities on the head. The theory was unscientific and was later determined to have no bearing on psychological characteristics of people. **(History)**

2. A neuron is also known as a nerve cell. The neuron is the fundamental building block of the nervous system, and each is composed of numerous dendrites, a cell body, and one axon. A myelin sheath covers the axon and helps transmit the messages faster. Myelin continues to grow throughout childhood. **(Components of neural system)**

3. The central nervous system consists of all the neurons, called interneurons, in the brain and in the spinal cord. **(Components of neural system)**

4. The peripheral nervous system consists of the neurons that connect the central nervous system to the rest of the body, including the sense receptors, muscles, and glands, by means of two divisions, the skeletal (somatic) and autonomic nervous systems. The skeletal nervous system controls voluntary movements of the skeletal muscles, while the autonomic nervous system controls the glands and muscles of the internal organs. **(Components of neural system)**

5. The divisions of the autonomic nervous system are the sympathetic and parasympathetic nervous systems. The sympathetic nervous system arouses the body, preparing it in stressful, emergency situations, by accelerating the heart, slowing digestion, and causing perspiration. The parasympathetic nervous system, in contrast, calms the body and helps it to relax by producing the opposite effects. **(Components of neural system)**

6. An action potential is a neural impulse that travels down an axon in the form of a brief electrical charge. An action potential takes place, in an all-or-none way, when the excitatory signals minus the inhibitory signals that enter the neuron via the dendrites exceed the threshold of the neuron. Gates in the axon open up and positively charged atoms move inside it, depolarizing part of the axon, and causing the next channel to open, thus creating an electrical chain reaction along the axon. **(Communication of neurons)**

7. Neurons, or nerve cells, communicate by means of action potentials. When the action potential comes to the end of the axon, or terminal knob, neurotransmitters are released into the synaptic gap between the sending and receiving neuron. The neurotransmitter molecules bind to receptor sites on the receiving neuron and have either an excitatory or inhibitory influence, affecting the receiving neuron's ability to create an action potential. **(Communication of neurons)**

8. The simplest nerve pathway is that of the reflex. It is important because it allows the body to respond in a simple, automatic way that is inborn in the animal or person. The reflex is processed by interneurons in the spinal cord, such that the body can respond quickly, even before the neural message continues on up to the brain for interpretation. Examples of reflexes are the response of pulling one's hand off a hot stove, the knee jerk to a doctor's mallet, and the eye blink in response to a puff of air. **(Reflexes)**

9. Neurotransmitters are chemical messengers that cross the synaptic gaps from the terminal ends of neurons and bind to the receptor sites on the receiving neurons, serving to determine whether a neural signal will be created or not. **(Neurotransmitters)**

10. Acetylcholine is a neurotransmitter that is realeased at every synaptic gap between a motor neuron and a muscle. Normally, it causes the muscle fibers to contract, so that physical movement can occur. However, a bite by the black widow spider causes a flood of acetylcholine, creating violent muscular contractions. On the other hand, curare and botulin block the transmission of acetylcholine, causing paralysis. Another class of neurotransmitters, endorphins, are similar to morphine, in that they are released in the brain in response to pain and hard exercise. Endorphins help in the understanding of the "runner's high," pain-relieving effects of acupuncture, and the ability to temporarily carry on without pain in the case of major bodily injury. Opiate drugs, such as heroin, can cause the brain to stop producing endorphins, so that the body comes to rely on heroin, and excessive pain and suffering occur when the person tries to give up the drug. Levels of dopamine in the brain can also influence behavior. Excessive dopamine is related to schizophrenia, whereas a lack is associated with Parkinson's disease. (**Neurotransmitters**)

11. Sensory neurons, also called afferent neurons, carry messages to the central nervous system from the sensory receptors, such as the pressure and temperature receptors in the skin. (**Types of neurons**)

12. In contrast, motor neurons, or efferent neurons, carry information in the opposite direction, from the central nervous system to the muscles and glands of the body, by means of separate neural pathways. (**Types of neurons**)

13. The endocrine system is a chemical communication system of glands—such as the pituitary gland, adrenal glands, ovaries, and testicles—that release hormones into the blood. The hormones are carried in the blood and influence growth, reproduction, reactions to stress, metabolism, and mood. The endocrine system works in a comparatively slow manner compared to neurons. (**Endocrine system**)

14. The pituitary gland, at the base of the brain, releases hormones that influence growth and also influence the release of other hormones, such as in the ovaries and testicles. The pituitary gland is part of the endocrine system. (**Endocrine system**)

15. The first techniques to discover brain functionality included examination of observable behavior as a result of brain diseases, injury to the brain, and autopsy. Electrical, chemical, and magnetic stimulation are more recent techniques used to study the brains of humans. The EEG, or electroencephalogram, records the brain's electrical activity from electrodes placed on the skull. The brain can also be examined by means of CAT (Computerized Axial Tomography) scans and the MRI (Magnetic Resonance Imaging) technique. (**Scientific study of the brain**)

16. The brain stem is the most primitive and innermost part of the brain. It begins where the spinal cord enters the skull. It contains components that monitor breathing and other basic bodily functions. (**Components of the brain**)

17. The structures within the brain stem are the medulla, the reticular formation, and the thalamus. (**Components of the brain**)

18. The medulla controls the beat of the heart. It also controls breathing, making it automatic. The medulla is the point where nerves from the body cross over to the opposite side of the brain. (**Components of the brain**)

19. The reticular formation is a finger-shaped network of neurons that controls the arousal of the organism, allowing the person or animal to pay attention to incoming sensory information. (**Components of the brain**)

20. The thalamus is like a telephone operator, as it serves to direct, or route, incoming information from the sensory neurons to the appropriate higher brain region of the cortex, such that the information can be interpreted in the part of the cortex that handles visual, auditory, taste, or touch information, accordingly. **(Components of the brain)**

21. The cerebellum is composed of two, wrinkled hemispheres that extend from the back of the brain stem. The term means "little brain." The cerebellum affects balance and coordinates voluntary movement, such as walking or reaching with a hand, making the motion smooth, rather than jerky. The cerebellum also plays a role in learning and memory. **(Components of the brain)**

22. The limbic system is a donut-shaped, neural system that influences emotions and motivations. Two components are the amygdala and hypothalamus. **(Components of the brain)**

23. The amygdala consists of two, almond-shaped clusters of neurons that are responsible for the expression of fear, rage, and aggression. Research has shown that the destruction of the amygdala can transform a normal housecat into an aggressive animal. In contrast, it has also been found that damage to the amygdala in violent monkeys can transform them into peaceful, calm animals. **(Components of the brain)**

24. The hypothalamus lies underneath the thalamus; therefore, its name, given that "hypo" means "below." The hypothalamus monitors hormone levels in the blood. Various neural clusters within the hypothalamus influence thirst, hunger, sexual behavior, and body temperature. So-called "pleasure centers" were first identified in the hypothalamus of rats by Olds and Milner in 1954. The hypothalamus can also activate autonomic nervous system activity. **(Components of the brain)**

25. Cortex means "bark." Mammals have larger, more developed cortical areas than do amphibians. The cerebral cortex allows for the ability to be adaptable to the environment, as a result of learning and thinking, rather than relying primarily on inborn knowledge. The cortex consists of two halves, or hemispheres, in a neural layer only 1/8 inch thick. It has a wrinkled appearance within the skull. The number of neurons in the cortex is estimated to be approximately 30 billion. Each brain hemisphere is composed of four areas, or lobes. **(Cortex)**

26. (a) The frontal lobes are positioned behind the forehead and are primarily involved in higher thought processes, such as planning and reasoning, and in the nature of personality. The motor cortex can be found in the frontal lobes. (b) The temporal lobes are located just above the ears. They are involved in interpretation of auditory information. Each temporal lobe receives information from the opposite ear. (c) The parietal lobes are located at the top and to the rear of the cortex and are also involved in higher thought processes. The parietal lobes are probably the least well understood of all the cortical areas, but it is known that the sensory cortex is located in the parietal lobes. (d) Finally, the two occipital lobes are at the back of the head. The occipital lobes are primarily responsible for the interpretation of visual information. **(Components of the brain)**

27. In the 1800s, railroad worker Phineas Gage was the victim of an accident, in which an explosion shot a tamping iron through his frontal lobe. Amazingly, he survived, but as a result, his personality became hostile and uncharacteristically aggressive. He also lost his job as foreman, because his ability to plan was affected. The accident provided scientists with the very first knowledge about the function of the frontal lobes. **(History)**

28. The motor cortex is located in the frontal lobes, directly in front of the central fissure, or main groove, between the frontal lobes and parietal lobes. The motor cortex sends messages out to the body, and thereby controls voluntary muscle movements. The motor cortex was mapped out by neuroscientist

Delgado, who discovered that each section is responsible for the control and movement of various body parts, such as the toes, arms, fingers, eyes, lips, and tongue. Damage to the motor cortex results in the inability to move the associated part of the body. Neurosurgeon Penfield found that direct stimulation of the motor cortex caused a person to move the corresponding body part, even if he or she tried as hard as possible not to move. (**Components of the brain**)

29. The sensory cortex is parallel to the motor cortex and is located just behind the central fissure, at the front of the parietal lobes. It receives information from the skin senses. Similar to the motor cortex, it can be mapped out. Such mapping shows that various parts of the sensory cortex are responsible for the ability to feel sensations in associated parts of the skin. For example, part of the sensory cortex processes incoming information from the toes, from the leg, from the hand, from the lips, etc. Therefore, it allows one to sense a touch on the hand versus a touch on the face. Neurosurgeon Penfield found that direct stimulation of the sensory cortex caused a person to feel as though the corresponding body part were actually being touched. The larger the section of sensory cortex devoted to a region of the body, the greater the sensitivity of the body region. (**Components of the brain**)

30. Damage to any of several areas in the cortex can cause an impairment in language ability. For example, damage to Broca's area in the left frontal lobe affects the ability to speak. Damage to Wernicke's area in the left temporal lobe inhibits the ability to comprehend language. Words can be spoken but they are meaningless. Finally, damage to the angular gyrus affects the ability to read aloud. (**Language processing**)

31. Approximately 95 percent of people who are right-handed process speech in the left hemisphere, but in left-handed people, about half process speech in the left hemisphere, one-quarter process it in the right hemisphere, and the remaining quarter of left-handed people process speech in both hemispheres. (**Language processing**)

32. A split brain is a brain that has had the two hemispheres, or halves, disconnected by means of cutting the corpus callosum. The corpus callosum consists of the wide band of nerve fibers that allows the two halves of the brain to communicate with each other. Split-brain surgery has been used to control severe epileptic seizures in patients who do not respond well to medicine for seizures. Cutting the corpus callosum prevents the seizures from moving across to the other hemisphere. It was discovered by Sperry, Myers, and Gazzaniga that split-brain patients showed certain behavioral abnormalities, and as a result, they discovered that the left and right hemispheres each have special functions. In most people, information in the left or right side of the visual field of both eyes will project to the opposite hemisphere of the brain through the corpus callosum. However, in the split-brain patient, the visual information cannot cross over. Given that the language centers are typically in the left hemisphere, a problem was created for the split-brain patient, when visual information was flashed to only the left or right side of the visual field. The result was that the split-brain patient was be unable either to recognize the flashed image or to say what the image was. Research on split-brain patients provided information on the functions of the two hemispheres in normal people. (**Split-brain research**)

Grade Yourself

Circle the numbers of the questions you missed, then fill in the total incorrect for each topic. If you answered more than three questions incorrectly, you need to focus on that topic. (If a topic has less than three questions and you had at least one wrong, we suggest you study that topic also. Read your textbook, a review book, or ask your teacher for help.)

Subject: Biological Psychology

Topic	Question Numbers	Number Incorrect
History	1, 27	
Components of neural system	2, 3, 4, 5	
Communication of neurons	6, 7	
Reflexes	8	
Neurotransmitters	9, 10	
Types of neurons	11, 12	
Endocrine system	13, 14	
Scientific study of the brain	15	
Components of the brain	16, 17, 18, 19, 20, 21, 22, 23, 24, 26, 28, 29	
Cortex	25	
Language processing	30, 31	
Split-brain research	32	

Sensation

5

Brief Yourself

Sensation describes the means by which people detect physical energy coming from the environment and then encode it as neural signals in the body, allowing the neural signals to travel to the brain for interpretation. The senses include vision, audition (hearing), taste, touch, smell, and the sense of equilibrium, or balance.

Test Yourself

1. What is an absolute threshold?

2. What is the process of signal detection?

3. What does sensory adaptation refer to?

4. Why is sensory adaptation beneficial?

5. What is the process that light follows from the surface of the eye to the retina?

6. What does the retina consist of?

7. How are the rods and cones different?

8. Where are most rods located? Where are most cones located?

9. What is the blind spot? Why is one unable to see anything there?

10. Where in the brain is visual information processed? Where is auditory information processed?

11. Explain the process of dark adaptation.

12. What is the Young-Helmholtz theory of color vision?

13. Describe the opponent process theory of color vision.

14. What do decibels measure?

15. Name the components of the outer ear.

16. What is the function of the outer ear?

17. What are the components of the middle ear?

18. What is the function of the middle ear?

19. What is found in the inner ear?

20. How does the cochlea function?

21. Name two theories of pitch perception, and explain each.

22. How do humans locate sounds?

23. Compare conduction deafness with nerve deafness.

24. What are the treatments for conduction deafness?

25. What are the treatments for nerve deafness?

26. How does the sense of hearing change over the lifespan?

27. What are the types of sensory receptors in the skin?

28. Explain the gate-control theory of pain.

29. What are the four basic taste sensations?

30. What type of sense is taste? How do taste receptors basically function?

31. How can the sense of taste be diminished? Describe at least two ways.

32. What is sensory interaction? What senses does it apply to?

33. Where are the sensory receptors for smell located?

34. What is the name for the sense that monitors position and movement of individual body parts? Where are these sensory receptors located?

35. What is the name for the sense that monitors position and movement and position of the body as a whole? Where are these sensory receptors located?

36. What does sensory deprivation involve? Describe the potential psychological effects.

Check Yourself

1. An absolute threshold refers to the minimum amount of a stimulus energy necessary to be able to detect the environmental stimulus 50 percent of the time. Below that level, stimuli are said to be subliminal. **(Psychophysics)**

2. The process of signal detection is that of picking up a signal from the environment. The threshold is not a constant. Instead, it depends on the strength of the stimulus, the experience of the person, and the person's expectations and possible fatigue. An applied example is that of monitoring radar. Performance of the technician depends on a number of variables that can be mathematically specified. **(Psychophysics)**

3. Sensory adaptation refers to a person's decreasing awareness of a stimulus that remains constant. For example, after putting on a watch, one quickly forgets it is there. One also adapts to the odor of one's own house, even if visitors might think the place smells of a dog. Similarly, one gets used to the light scent of perfume on the person seated next to him or her in a theater. **(Psychophysics)**

4. Sensory adaptation is beneficial because it allows the brain to focus attention on informative changes in the environment and process them, as opposed to being distracted by uninformative stimuli that are constant. **(Psychophysics)**

5. In the process of vision, light enters the eye through the sclera and next moves through the cornea, which slightly bends the rays. Next, light waves move through the opening of the eye called the pupil. The diameter of the pupil is controlled by the layers of the surrounding iris. The light continues on and passes through the gel-filled lens, which accommodates, or changes shape, to allow the focus of the light on the retina at the back of the eye. **(The eye)**

6. The retina, which lines the back of the eye, consists of rods and cones where the light is transformed into neural energy, plus ganglion and bipolar cells. The retina is considered to be part of the central nervous system. **(The eye)**

7. The rods allow processing under dim levels of illumination, whereas the cones allow visual processing under bright illumination. Cones also allow us to see fine detail and color. **(The eye)**

8. Most of the rods are located in the periphery of the retina, whereas the cones are densely concentrated in the center of the retina in an area called the fovea. There are approximately 120 million rods but only 6 million cones. **(The eye)**

9. The blind spot is the point for each eye at which the optic nerve leaves the retina and proceeds on to the occipital lobes. One is unable to see anything at the location of each blind spot because there are no sensory receptors (rods or cones) at this point. **(The eye)**

10. Visual information is processed and interpreted in the occipital lobes of the cortex. Auditory information is interpreted in the temporal lobes. **(Sensory information processing)**

11. The process of dark adaptation takes about fifteen to twenty minutes to occur completely. It happens when one moves from a brightly lit area into a dimly lit place. The reason dark adaptation takes time is because the processing is transferred over from the cones to the rods. Light adaptation is the opposite of dark adaptation. **(Dark/light adaptation)**

12. The Young-Helmholtz theory of color vision is a trichromatic theory. It says that the retina has three different types of color receptors, and each one is sensitive to either red, green, or blue. To be able to see other colors, combinations of those three color receptors must be activated. For example, to experience yellow, our red and green receptors must be stimulated. **(Theories of color vision)**

13. The opponent process theory of color vision states that at the level of the thalamus in the brain, visual information is analyzed according to opposing colors, such as red/green, black/white, and blue/yellow. The theory explains why people see the particular colors of afterimages that they do, such as after staring at a colored drawing of a red, white, and blue American flag and then looking away to a white surface and seeing a yellow, green, and black flag. **(Theories of color vision)**

14. Decibels measure sound energy, and the absolute threshold for audition is defined as zero decibels. **(Properties of sound)**

15. The components of the outer ear are pinna, or fleshy part of the ear, and the auditory canal. **(The ear)**

16. The function of the outer ear is to capture the sound waves and funnel them into the auditory canal, so that they hit the ear drum and can be magnified. **(The ear)**

17. The ear drum separates the outer ear from the middle ear. The components of the middle ear are the three bones called the hammer, anvil, and stirrup. These are the smallest bones in the body. They chain together. The hammer is moved by the vibrating ear drum. The anvil is moved by the vibrating hammer. In turn, the anvil causes the stirrup to move, and that vibrates the membrane of the oval window. **(The ear)**

18. The function of the middle ear is to amplify, or increase, the sound vibrations. **(The ear)**

19. The oval window separates the middle ear from the inner ear. The snail-shaped cochlea is contained in the inner ear. **(The ear)**

20. The cochlea is filled with fluid. Vibrations in the fluid cause the hair cells that line the basilar membrane to bend. The bending action starts neural impulses in the nearby nerve fibers, transforming the sound waves into neural signals. The individual nerve fibers bundle together as the auditory nerve and continue on to the temporal lobes of the cortex. **(The ear)**

21. One theory of pitch perception is place theory. According to place theory, different frequencies start neural activity at different physical places along the basilar membrane. The brain is able to determine the pitch of the sound, according to the location on the membrane from which the signal came. Another theory of pitch perception is frequency theory. According to frequency theory, the auditory nerve creates neural impulses at the same rate as the frequency of the sound. It turns out that a combination of the two theories can best explain hearing. **(Theories of pitch perception)**

22. Humans locate sounds by means of the brief time delay when the signal reaches the first ear and when it reaches the second. A sound coming from one side will reach one ear first and will be slightly louder. However, that creates a difficulty in determining the location of a sound that comes from directly behind, beneath, or overhead, as such sounds arrive at the ears simultaneously. **(Location of sound)**

23. Conduction deafness involves damage to the ear drum or to the bones of the middle ear, while nerve deafness involves damage to the hair cells that line the basilar membrane of the cochlea. **(Deafness)**

24. Conduction deafness is a problem with the mechanical system that conducts sound waves. Treatments for conduction deafness involve the use of hearing aids that amplify the sound. **(Deafness)**

25. Nerve deafness is more serious than conduction deafness. Treatments for nerve deafness include surgery, but sometimes there is no cure. Nerve deafness can result from prolonged exposure to loud noises, as a result of disease, or simply due to aging. **(Deafness)**

26. Over one's lifespan, the sense of hearing becomes less acute. Men typically start to lose hearing before women do. It is the high tones that tend to disappear first. Thus, a man in his forties might start to have difficulty hearing the doorbell. **(Deafness)**

27. The sensory receptors in the skin include pressure, cold, warmth, and pain. These receptors allow humans to experience the entire array of sensations. **(Sensation)**

28. The gate-control theory of pain involves the idea that the spinal cord contains a neural-type gate that can open, allowing pain signals to go to the brain, or that close, to block them. This theory partially explains why therapies such as massage, acupuncture and electrical stimulation might relieve chronic pain. **(Pain)**

29. The four basic taste sensations are sweet, sour, salty, and bitter. **(Sensation)**

30. Taste is a chemical sense. The taste receptors function because of a breakdown of the food molecules. The taste buds are spread unevenly across the tongue, so certain parts of the tongue are more sensitive to some tastes than others. For example, the tip of the tongue is most sensitive to sweetness. **(Sensation)**

31. The sense of taste is diminished by activities such as smoking and the use of alcohol. Also, taste buds continually die and replace themselves about every seven days, but as a person gets older, the process of replacement becomes less efficient. As people age, taste becomes less sensitive. **(Sensation)**

32. Sensory interaction is the fact that one sense can affect another sense. It applies to the relationship between taste and smell, and between taste and vision, for example. When a person has a head cold, smell is diminished, and therefore taste is dulled as a result. Similarly, if food, such as spaghetti, is colored blue, it won't taste as good as if it were the traditional color. **(Sensory interaction)**

33. The sensory receptors for smell are located high up in the nose in the olfactory bulbs. Molecules are carried through the air and are pulled up to the olfactory bulbs through the nasal cavity passages when one inhales. How the olfactory receptors work has not yet been completely determined by scientists. **(Sensation)**

34. The sense that monitors position and movement of individual body parts is called kinesthesis. These sensory receptors are located in the tendons, muscles, and joints. **(Kinesthesis)**

35. The sense that monitors position and movement of the entire body is called equilibrium. These sensory receptors are located inside the inner ear, in the semicircular canals and in the vestibular sacs. They also allow a person to keep his or her balance. **(Equilibrium)**

36. Sensory deprivation has been created in experimental settings by keeping a person from experiencing incoming sensory input. This can be arranged by wearing goggles that block out light, wearing special skin covering to block the sensation of touch, and being put in a silent room for an extended period of time. If a person experiences complete sensory deprivation, he or she will begin to hallucinate. However, if sensory input is merely restricted and minimized, most people find it significantly reduces stress and can aid in the process of behavior modification, such as to stop smoking. **(Sensory deprivation)**

Grade Yourself

Circle the numbers of the questions you missed, then fill in the total incorrect for each topic. If you answered more than three questions incorrectly, you need to focus on that topic. (If a topic has less than three questions and you had at least one wrong, we suggest you study that topic also. Read your textbook, a review book, or ask your teacher for help.)

Subject: Sensation

Topic	Question Numbers	Number Incorrect
Psychophysics	1, 2, 3, 4	
The eye	5, 6, 7, 8, 9	
Sensory information processing	10	
Dark/light adaptation	11	
Theories of color vision	12, 13	
Properties of sound	14	
The ear	15, 16, 17, 18, 19, 20	
Theories of pitch perception	21	
Location of sound	22	
Deafness	23, 24, 25, 26	
Sensation	27, 29, 30, 31, 33	
Pain	28	
Sensory interaction	32	
Kinesthesis	34	
Equilibrium	35	
Sensory deprivation	36	

Perception

6

Brief Yourself

A sensation is the automatic response of a sense organ to a stimulus from the outside world. Perception is a (mentally) active process in which we code the sensory data, integrate it, and give it meaning; it is via perception that we are aware of the things or entities "out there." The faculty of perception is what allows us to retain "memories" of sensations. Some characteristics of perception are biological, built into our nervous system, while others result from learning—our expectations, emotions, and needs. Whereas the process of sensation is wholly automatic, perception is subject to our control through how we direct our attention — the stimuli we select to devote our cognitive resources to.

Test Yourself

1. Define attention.

2. What role does attention play in perception?

3. What are the characteristics of stimuli that attract our attention?

4. What is shadowing, and how does it explain the "cocktail party phenomenon"?

5. What role does "perceptual set" play in perception?

6. How do figure-ground relations affect perception?

7. Provide brief definitions for the Gestalt principles of similarity, proximity, closure, and continuity.

8. What is a perceptual schema?

9. Give an example of perceptual adaptation.

10. What is the difference between bottom-up and top-down processing?

11. What is a geon?

12. In terms of hypothesis testing, what is an illusion?

13. What are perceptual constancies? Give examples of several different types.

14. Give several examples of how different monocular cues provide us with depth information.

15. What is stereopsis?

16. When we perceive smooth motion, do the sensory stimuli truly have to be continuous?

17. What do people blind from birth "see" when their vision is restored in adulthood?

18. Give an example of how "critical periods" affect perceptual development.

19. Do we benefit from pain? Explain.

20. What are endorphins?

21. What strategies might help us cope with pain?

Check Yourself

1. Attention refers to the stimuli that are in our awareness, and it involves two processes of selection: focusing on certain stimuli (bringing into or keeping them in our awareness), and filtering out others (excluding them from our awareness). While millions of sensory messages may be being processed by our sense organs and sent on for further perceptual integration by our cognitive faculties, we become "aware" of only a small proportion. **(Attention)**

2. Where we direct our attention determines the stimuli we process first as sensations, then integrate as perceptions. If while driving we direct our attention to the road straight ahead and ignore cross-street traffic, we will likely have an accident. **(Attention)**

3. Stimuli that are meaningful to us, such as advertisements that appeal to a personal interest, attract our attention. Stimulus characteristics such as movement, intensity, novelty, contrast, and repetition, also affect whether we will notice them or not. **(Attention)**

4. Shadowing is a technique used in experiments in which people hear two messages simultaneously through headphones, one in each ear. Subjects asked to shadow one of the messages repeat it word for word as they listen; when they do this, they are unable to remember what the other message was about. Alternatively, subjects are able to switch their attention between both messages and understand them well enough to get the gist of what they are about. The conclusion is that we cannot attend completely to more than one thing at a time but are able to shift our attention rapidly. **(Attention)**

5. A perceptual set is a readiness to perceive stimuli in a certain way. If we are alone walking down a dimly lit street at night and we see shadows following us, we immediately conclude a thug is waiting to mug us when it may be nothing more than a cat out for a nightly stroll. The sensory stimulation in both situations may be the same, but the identification process of our perception is influenced by the surrounding environment and our expectations. **(Perceptual set)**

6. Figure-ground relations are how we organize the stimuli into a central, or foreground, figure, and a background. Reversible figures are those which can be seen in two different ways depending on which aspect is selected as figure (and ground). For example, the drawing of a vase or two faces in profile is a common deception of figure-ground relations. **(Figure-ground)**

7. These Gestalt principles all pertain to how we group and interpret stimuli. Similarity: if figures are similar to each other, such as the same shape (triangle, circle), we will group them together. Proximity: elements or figures near each other will be perceived as parts of a larger array, not as separate elements. Closure: mentally closing of gaps or openings in an element, such as seeing a series of dashed lines arranged in a continuous arc as a circle, or when arranged in a row as a long line. Continuity: linking individual elements so they form a continuous line or pattern that makes sense. **(Grouping stimuli)**

8. A perceptual schema is a complex information structure that contains the critical features of objects, events, and other perceptual phenomena. The schema is the internal representation that allows us to classify sensory data and make instantaneous perceptual judgments. For instance, whom to greet when we arrive home at the end of the day, our roommate, our dog, or our cat. The features of the incoming stimuli are somehow compared with various internal representations until a best fit is established, and this is whom we say "Hi!" to. **(Perceptual schema)**

9. Perceptual adaptation is the ability to adjust to an artificially distorted sensory data stream. For example, people can adapt to glasses that invert (turn the visual field upside-down), or offset it 40 degrees to the

left or right. Hearing aids sometimes sound "tinny," yet wearers quickly learn to recognize the (new) sound of their friends' voices. **(Perceptual adaptation)**

10. Bottom-up and top-down processing are two fundamentally different approaches to processing sensory information. With bottom-up processing, the individual elements are inspected and combined to produce our perception; it begins with basic-level elements progressively integrated into larger structures until what is perceived somehow matches what "out there." Top-down processing is a hypothesis-driven approach that interprets the sensory stimuli in light of perceptual schemas and the meaning associated with them. The Gestalt principles are an example of top-down processing. **(Theories of processing sensory information)**

11. A geon is a basic three-dimensional geometric form used in visual object recognition. These twenty-five to thirty-five forms can be combined to create the shape of any object that can exist. Geons are an element of a proposed recognition by components theory for how bottom-up processing might occur. **(Theories of processing sensory information)**

12. In terms of hypothesis testing, an illusion is an incorrect hypothesis. Particularly in top-down processing, if we expect one thing but perceive another, the hypothesis is in error. Another interpretation is that an illusion is an incorrect perception. For example, a straight stick half in and half out of the water appears to bend sharply just below the surface; the water is not causing the stick to bend, but water and air diffract light waves differently, thus leading to the illusion. **(Illusions)**

13. Perceptual constancies are the brain's ability to perceive two identical stimuli under changed conditions as the same. Size constancy, for instance, is knowing how large a car is, whether seen in our driveway or from an airplane. Shape constancy allows us to recognize a car from many different angles. Color constancy is the ability to "see" the same color under different lighting conditions, such as a piece of yellow notebook paper in bright sunlight, under fluorescent lighting, or in a dimly lit coffee shop. **(Perceptual constancy)**

14. Visual cues that provide us with depth information and require only one eye are called monocular cues. Linear perspective is one such cue, such as parallel railroad tracks seeming to angle closer together as they recede in the distance. The three remaining distance cues are height in the horizontal plane, texture, and clarity. Two other cues are light and shadow, as in many of the works by M.C. Escher, and interposition, when a closer object cuts off our view of a more distant object. **(Depth perception)**

15. Stereopsis is the appearance of depth that results from the use of both eyes. These binocular cues lead to binocular disparity wherein each eye sees a slightly different image. These images are fused by higher levels of the visual system and provide us with the appearance of depth. **(Depth perception)**

16. No. Stroboscopic movement is the principle behind moving pictures, which is a series of still photographs projected on a screen in rapid succession. A theater marquee that has lights that seem to move endlessly around them or spell out a message are examples of still images perceived as continuous motion. **(Perception of motion)**

17. Research on this has been with people born with congenital cataracts; they are able to perceive light but not patterns or shapes. When their vision is restored they can follow moving targets, scan objects visually, and perceive figure-ground relations. On the other hand, they cannot visually identify objects they were familiar with through touch. Perceptual constancy is poor, and even years after their vision was restored, they could only recognize the faces of people they knew well. They are also poor at judging distances. **(Perceptual development)**

18. Critical periods are times during which certain kinds of experiences must occur if perceptual abilities are to develop normally. People born with congenital cataracts and unable to see anything but light or dark, who later have their vision restored, never achieve full development of their visual system compared to a normally sighted person. Experiments with kittens raised in a vertical or horizontal striped chamber show that they do not develop cells in the visual cortex that fire in response to horizontal or vertical stimuli, respectively. **(Perceptual development)**

19. Pain is our body's way of telling us something has gone wrong; thus pain has survival functions. It is a warning signal that draws our attention when some part of the body is being damaged or threatened. Pain is also part of the body's defensive system to help us cope with the threat by telling us to change our behavior. **(Pain)**

20. Endorphins are the nervous system's built-in painkillers, natural opiates that bind in regions of the brain associated with pain suppression and pleasure. Endorphins have been identified that are 200 times more powerful than morphine. **(Pain)**

21. Self-efficacy, the conviction that one can cope, is a major factor in pain tolerance. Dissociative strategies are those that distract you from the painful sensory input; the more concentration or cognitive activity required, the more effective they are. Associative strategies are the reverse; instead, you focus your attention on the physical sensations but in a detached and unemotional fashion. With associate strategies it is important to not label the sensations as painful or difficult to tolerate. Finally, with injury, it is important to return to activity as soon as the healing process will allow. Research shows that those who avoid activity or become overly protective are more likely to develop a chronic pain condition. Meditation and relaxation can also help one cope with pain. **(Pain)**

Grade Yourself

Circle the numbers of the questions you missed, then fill in the total incorrect for each topic. If you answered more than three questions incorrectly, you need to focus on that topic. (If a topic has less than three questions and you had at least one wrong, we suggest you study that topic also. Read your textbook, a review book, or ask your teacher for help.)

Subject: Perception

Topic	Question Numbers	Number Incorrect
Attention	1, 2, 3, 4	
Perceptual set	5	
Figure-ground	6	
Grouping stimuli	7	
Perceptual schema	8	
Perceptual adaptation	9	
Theories of processing sensory information	10, 11	
Illusions	12	
Perceptual constancy	13	
Depth perception	14, 15	
Perception of motion	16	
Perceptual development	17, 18	
Pain	19, 20, 21	

Learning

Brief Yourself

Learning is a relatively permanent change in behavior as a result of experience and involves changes in performance. A change in "potential" behavior is also learning and instead involves a change in knowledge. The neurological processes underlying learning are not observable, so it must be defined in terms of external, observable (potential) performance. All learning is associative learning, the linking of two events that occur close together. While most principles of learning have come from research on nonhuman subjects, they have been found to apply to people, too, and therefore have been adapted and applied to therapies aimed at changing human behavior.

Test Yourself

1. What are classical conditioning and operant conditioning?

2. To what does the term "stimulus substitution" refer in terms of classical conditioning?

3. Define acquisition, extinction, and spontaneous recovery in the classical conditioning paradigm.

4. What is the difference between generalization and discrimination?

5. What role does "predictability" play in classical conditioning?

6. What is the difference between an elicited behavior and an emitted behavior?

7. Define Thorndike's law of effect.

8. Explain operant conditioning.

9. In terms of operant conditioning, what is a reinforcer?

10. Define shaping.

11. What is a partial reinforcement schedule?

12. Define the four types of partial reinforcement schedules.

13. Are punishment and negative reinforcement the same? Explain.

14. What is avoidance learning, and why is it so difficult to unlearn?

15. What is "response cost" punishment?

16. Is aversive punishment an effective method of shaping behavior?

17. Classical conditioning has been explained in terms of cognition. How does this position differ from traditional explanations?

18. Does reinforcement always come from an external source, or can it be generated internally? Punishment?

19. How does observational learning, or modeling, differ from classical conditioning and operant conditioning?

20. Do the expected consequences affect performance for observationally learned behavior?

21. What is "preparedness," and what does it mean in terms of learning?

22. Can an animal be "conditioned" after only a single trial or single experience?

Check Yourself

1. Conditioning is the process of learning associations, that certain events occur together. Classical conditioning is associating two stimuli together, such as the click an alarm clock might make before the buzzer sounds (the two stimuli become associated). We immediately tense up or reach out (the response) for the clock at the sound of the click, even before the buzzer has sounded. (**Classical conditioning**)

2. Stimulus substitution is when a previously neutral stimulus is used in place of the original stimulus to elicit the desired response. This is what happens when the CR takes the place of the UCR to bring about the CS/UCS. (**Classical conditioning**)

3. Acquisition is the learning phase of classical conditioning, when the CS and UCS are paired to strengthen the association between them. Extinction is the process of weakening the CS–CR bond when the CS is repeatedly presented without the subsequent UCS; the CR will eventually disappear. Spontaneous recovery is the sudden reappearance of the CR after it has been extinguished. This can occur if the CS is presented after a rest period following extinction, although the CS will usually be weaker. (**Classical conditioning**)

4. Stimulus generalization is responding to a similar CS. For example, if the telephone rings when we are visiting friends, we initially start to answer it even though the ringing is very different from our own telephone. Stimulus discrimination is the reverse situation when we detect differences in the stimuli, such as the different ringing patterns for each incoming line on our telephone. (**Generalization, discrimination**)

5. Predictability is the basis of the association between the UCS and the CS. What is important for an animal's learning of this bond is not how often the UCS follows the CS, but how reliably the CS predicts the UCS—in other words, how often the tone predicts the meal. (**Classical conditioning**)

6. An elicited behavior is one that is triggered by a specific event, a CR triggering a CS. An emitted behavior is one of many behaviors in a situation with many stimuli; it is "natural" in that the organism is the one choosing when and how to respond. Operant conditioning is the selective reinforcement of a particular behavior. (**Conditioning**)

7. Thorndike's law of effect can be summarized as: rewarded behavior is likely to recur. In other words, if a response is followed by a pleasant consequence, the likelihood of that response occurring again will increase. And the reverse situation of a response followed by a negative consequence is less likely to happen again. The law of effect is the foundation of operant conditioning. (**Operant conditioning**)

8. Operant conditioning is the association of a response and its consequence, such as when praising a young child who has just taken his or her first step. In this example, the walking is the response, and the parent's praise and excitement are the consequence. It is a type of learning. Behavior is more likely to be repeated if followed by positive reinforcement, and less likely if followed by punishment. (**Operant conditioning**)

9. A reinforcer is anything that increases the likelihood of a particular response occurring again. Reinforcers are distinguished on two axes, positive or negative, and primary or secondary. Positive and negative are used in the mathematical sense (not as value judgments) to differentiate when a reinforcer is given (positive) or removed (negative). For instance, our paycheck at the end of the week is a positive reinforcer, while hitting the snooze bar on the alarm clock is a negative reinforcer because it takes away the buzzing. A primary reinforcer is one that satisfies a biological need such as food and water. A

secondary, or conditioned, reinforcer is one that does not directly satisfy a biological need and is learned, such as praise, attention, even baseball cards. **(Reinforcement)**

10. Shaping is the reinforcement of behaviors that are progressively closer to the desired behavior. It is also called the method of successive approximation because only behavior that becomes more like the end desired behavior is rewarded; in this sense the organism's performance must "improve." Shaping is how animals at the circus and in other shows are trained; tigers do not naturally jump through hoops, they must be taught to do this. **(Shaping)**

11. A partial reinforcement schedule is one in which only some of the responses are reinforced, also called an intermittent reinforcement schedule. In contrast, a continuous reinforcement schedule rewards every response of a particular type. **(Reinforcement)**

12. Partial reinforcement schedules are categorized as ratio or interval, and fixed or variable. With ratio schedules a certain percentage of responses is reinforced (say, every tenth one), and in an interval schedule a certain amount of time must elapse between responses, regardless of the number of responses. A fixed schedule produces a reinforcement after a preset number of responses (fixed ratio) or a set period of time (fixed interval). On a variable schedule the behavior is reinforced after an unpredictable number of responses varying around an average (variable ratio), or around an unpredictable period of time varying around an average (variable interval). People who gamble are rewarded on a variable-ratio schedule. **(Reinforcement)**

13. No. Although these two are often confused, their effects on learning are actually the opposite of each other. Whereas negative reinforcement increases the likelihood of a behavior by removing something (hitting the snooze bar to shut off the alarm), punishment "decreases" the likelihood of a behavior (being chewed out because we are late to work). Both positive and negative reinforcement increase the likelihood of a behavior by "rewarding" it; punishment decreases the likelihood of a behavior by associating unpleasant or otherwise painful consequences with it. **(Negative reinforcement vs. punishment)**

14. Avoidance learning is identifying a discriminative stimulus that precedes something unpleasant and using it to avoid the unpleasant event. For example, you meet someone you are attracted to but also feel nervous and unsure of yourself around him or her, so instead you remain with your friends, with whom you feel comfortable and at ease. This is avoidance conditioning, and it is so difficult to unlearn because you are constantly "rewarded" by staying with your friends and not seeking out new people — you never take the step to find out if you are still nervous around potential new friends. **(Avoidance learning)**

15. Response cost punishment is the taking away of positive reinforcers, such as social interactions or possessions. It differs from aversive punishment in that this latter type is the application of an aversive stimulus, such as being reprimanded for being late to work. **(Punishment)**

16. In general, aversive punishment is not an effective form of shaping behavior because it only inhibits or suppresses the behavior that preceded it; it does not eliminate it. The problems associated with this method of controlling behavior are that it may be temporary and last only as long as the punisher is present; the punishment may become associated with the punisher instead of the undesired behavior; strong punishment can generalize to other behaviors that are actually appropriate; punishment also arouses negative emotions that can be upsetting to all. Aversive punishment also sets an example — especially relevant with children — that it is appropriate to control behavior through aggression; research has shown that such children in day-care centers display more aggression than those who do not receive severe physical punishment. **(Types of punishment)**

17. The traditional view of classical conditioning was that of learning a simple association between the UCS and CS. In terms of cognition, what is most important is how reliably the UCS follows the CS; it is the expectancy—the predictability of the UCS from the CS—that matters, not the mere frequency of pairing. Further support for the cognitive role comes from experiments on the phenomenon known as "blocking," in which a second CS presented simultaneously with the first CS fails to become associated with the UCS. Traditional classical conditioning theory cannot explain this, whereas the cognitive approach says that because the second CS does not enhance the predictability of the UCS, no association will be formed. **(Cognition and classical conditioning)**

18. Self-evaluative processes are how we evaluate our behavior according to our own internal standards. As children we learn these standards from significant adults such as parents and teachers; they reward us with their approval when we meet their standards, and disapprove of us when we do not. As we grow up we may adopt these standards as our own, or learn new ones by observing others or thinking about what our standards should be. We then use these standards as a basis for self-evaluation and can either praise or chastise ourselves accordingly. **(Reinforcement)**

19. Whereas classical conditioning and operant conditioning both rely solely on experience to form associations, modeling posits that associations can be learned by observing others, with the performance — the observable and measurable aspect of learning — becoming apparent sometime later when the behavior is imitated. **(Observational learning)**

20. Yes. While the behavior can be learned merely by observing a model, whether it is eventually imitated or performed is largely due to the expected consequences. For example, if a child sees aggressive behavior punished, he or she is less likely to imitate it than when he or she sees that aggressive behavior has no effect or is rewarded. **(Observational learning)**

21. Preparedness is the construct that animals are biologically prepared to form associations between particular types of events, especially those that are adaptive and contribute to their survival as a species. For instance, it is relatively easy to teach a pigeon to peck at something to obtain food, and extremely difficult (if not impossible) instead to teach it to flap its wings to earn a seed. The first is an example of preparedness. **(Biological aspects of learning)**

22. Certain food aversions can be conditioned after only a single trial or experience. A rat that eats a food that makes it ill will associate the taste of that particular food with being sick and avoid it thereafter. With rats, taste can be conditioned this way, but odors cannot. Quail can develop an aversion based on the visual characteristics of food; even though they have a keen sense of taste, they do not learn aversions based on taste. **(Biological aspects of learning)**

Grade Yourself

Circle the numbers of the questions you missed, then fill in the total incorrect for each topic. If you answered more than three questions incorrectly, you need to focus on that topic. (If a topic has less than three questions and you had at least one wrong, we suggest you study that topic also. Read your textbook, a review book, or ask your teacher for help.)

Subject: Learning

Topic	Question Numbers	Number Incorrect
Classical conditioning	1, 2, 3, 5	
Generalization, discrimination	4	
Conditioning	6	
Operant conditioning	7, 8	
Reinforcement	9, 11, 12, 18	
Shaping	10	
Negative reinforcement vs. punishment	13	
Avoidance learning	14	
Punishment	15, 16	
Cognition and classical conditioning	17	
Observational learning	19, 20	
Biological aspects of learning	21, 22	

Memory

8

Brief Yourself

Memory refers to the processes that record information and to the experiences that can be later retrieved and/or expressed in behavior. Memory is viewed from three perspectives: content, processes, and architecture. The content of memory consists of three major systems, each referring to a different type of information: episodic, semantic, and procedural memory. The stages or processes of memory are the encoding, storage, and retrieval of information. The memory system's architecture is the structure of memory as utilized during the encoding, storage, and retrieval stages. Memory structure consists of the sensory registers, short-term or working memory, and long-term memory. Forgetting is the inability to retrieve information. Memory reconstruction is rebuilding an incomplete and sketchy memory with "reasonable" embellishments.

Test Yourself

1. Describe the contents of the three major memory systems.

2. What is the difference between procedural and declarative memory?

3. Describe the memory encoding process.

4. What is the difference between iconic and echoic memory?

5. Contrast implicit and explicit memory.

6. To what does the phrase "the magical number 7, plus or minus 2" refer?

7. What is chunking?

8. Contrast maintenance rehearsal with elaborative rehearsal.

9. What is the serial position curve, and how do the primacy effect and recency effect relate to it?

10. If in a list-learning experiment recall is delayed by about a minute, what happens to the primacy and recency effects? Why?

11. What are the differences between recall, recognition, and relearning measures of memory?

12. Discuss the relationship between priming and retrieval cues.

13. What is the interference theory of forgetting?

14. Compare motivated forgetting with repression.

15. Describe state-dependent memory and mood-congruent recall.

16. What role does distinctiveness play in retrieval, and how does it relate to "flashbulb" memory?

17. What is a mnemonic device? Give examples.

18. What are schemas and scripts, and what roles do they play in memory?

19. What are some ways to improve memory?

20. How reliable is eyewitness testimony?

Check Yourself

1. Episodic memory is the recollection of past personal experiences or episodes. It is personal, factual, and autobiographical. Semantic memory is general knowledge about the world including language. Procedural memory is our knowledge of how to accomplish tasks. It often involves motor skills such as in typing or riding a bicycle. (**Memory types**)

2. Declarative memory is episodic or semantic in nature and can be verbalized when recalled. Procedural memory is skill-based and is used for doing rather than describing. (**Memory types**)

3. Memory encoding is the first step in the memory process. It is the translation of incoming sensory information into a form the brain can process. After the sensory information has been encoded, it is sent to specific areas of the brain for further processing and integration with other information. Each sense is specially processed by one or more structures in the brain. (**Encoding**)

4. Iconic memory is the lingering or persistence of a visual image and lasts for a few tenths of a second. Echoic memory is the sensory store associated with hearing and lasts for two to four seconds. Each sensory system has its own storage system, and they are referred to collectively as "sensory stores." (**Memory types**)

5. Explicit memory refers to the conscious recollection of material, usually episodic or semantic in nature. Implicit memory refers to the retention of information in the absence of conscious attempts at recollection, that is, learned without conscious knowledge or effort. Although for explicit memory pictures are often retained better than words, this is not true with implicit memory. (**Memory types**)

6. Short-term memory has a limited capacity, a limit of about seven units of meaningful information. In contrast, long-term memory is believed to have unlimited capacity. (**Memory types**)

7. Chunking is the combining of individual items into a larger unit of meaning, such as seeing words instead of letters on this paper you are reading. Its purpose is to reduce the number of units active in memory at any one time. (**Chunking**)

8. Maintenance rehearsal is a method for keeping material active in short-term memory. Repeating a phone number to yourself before dialing it would be an example. Elaborative rehearsal focuses on the meaning of the information and relates it to other things we know. The purpose of elaborative rehearsal is to aid the transfer to long-term memory. While maintenance rehearsal strives for literal recall, elaborative rehearsal codes the general meaning of the information in memory, not the individual words. (**Rehearsal**)

9. The serial position curve refers to the U-shaped curve obtained in list-learning experiments. The shape of the curve is the percentage of words correctly recalled. The earliest and latest words presented are recalled best. The words in the middle of the list yield the poorest recall. The primacy effect refers to the recall of words at the beginning of the list. The superior recall of words presented at the end of the list is called the recency effect because they were the words presented most recently. (**Serial position effect**)

10. The primacy effect is largely unchanged. Recall of words from the end of the list, the recency effect, declines to the same level as words from the middle of the list. (**Serial position effect**)

11. Recall is retrieving information that is not in conscious awareness. Recognition is identifying previously learned information using environmental stimuli as retrieval cues. The difference is as that between an essay exam and a multiple-choice test. Relearning is a measure of the amount of time saved when

previously learned material is learned for a second time, then a third, and so on. Tests consistently show that people remember more than they can recall. This is why recognition tests of memory are "easier," because they provide retrieval cues that serve as aids to locate the information in memory. (**Recall vs. recognition**)

12. A retrieval cue is something that helps us bring a memory into consciousness from long-term memory. Priming is an example of how one cue can trigger associated elements in memory. Priming can be very specific, as in a multiple-choice test question and choosing the best answer. It can also be more general such as when you see a snow-capped mountain, this might partially activate concepts of skiing, shoveling driveways, and hot chocolate. This latter is known as "spreading activation." (**Retrieval cues**)

13. The interference theory of forgetting is the idea that memories cannot be retrieved because other information in memory is interfering with the retrieval process. The two most important types are proactive interference and retroactive interference. Proactive interference is when previously learned material interferes with material learned later; the direction of the interference is from older to newer. For example, for a few days after getting a new phone number, you start to give your old one to those who ask for it before you catch yourself. Retroactive interference is when newly learned material interferes with our ability to recall what we learned earlier; the direction of interference is from newer to older. An example of retroactive interference would be trying to recall a lecture from the beginning of the term compared to the one you just had. (**Forgetting**)

14. Motivated forgetting takes several forms. One is the irretrievability of memories that are shameful or embarrassing to remember. Freud's notion of repression is similar in that when a shocking or anxiety-arousing thought comes to mind, it is immediately pushed into the unconscious mind. The amnesia that people can suffer after a traumatic event is an exaggerated form of this. (**Forgetting**)

15. State-dependent memory refers to a person's internal physiological state at the time of learning, and that re-creating this state will prime recall. The internal "state" retrieval cues aid in the recall. Experimental results suggest that the phenomenon is unreliable. On the other hand, mood-congruent recall is a more consistent effect: people's recall is significantly improved when they are in the same mood as when they learned the information. People also tend to selectively remember happy events when they are happy, and sad events when they are sad. (**Mood and memory**)

16. Unexpected or unusual events are usually more easily recalled than commonplace ones. The distinctiveness of the event means there is little material in our memory to interfere with our recall of it. Flashbulb memories are those associated with a unique event, one that we have a strong emotional reaction to. Getting behind the steering wheel of a car for the first time is one for many of us. (**Flashbulb memories**)

17. A mnemonic device is a technique to improve memory. It typically involves two key features—a good recoding technique and effective retrieval cues. The Method of Loci and the Peg Method are two such techniques. An acronym can also provide retrieval cues, such as the first letter of the word to be remembered. (**Memory improvement**)

18. Sometimes what we construct in memory is not a precise record of the details of an episode but instead a broad-based theme that describes the meaning. The broad-based theme is the schema and often serves as an organizational device for how information is encoded and later recalled. Schemas are broader than concepts. A script is a specific type of schema for a particular activity, such as ordering in a restaurant. (**Memory construction**)

19. The most important principle to practice is to link the information together in a meaningful way and associate it with other items in memory. Spend more time and effort relating it to other items in memory and the environment. This will increase the number of available retrieval cues. Organize the material so you actively think about it and process it. Distribute the learning over time instead of all at once. **(Memory improvement)**

20. Remembering is often constructive and can be affected by the person asking the question. Research on eyewitness testimony shows that people will fill in missing details with consistent material and that details will often change on subsequent retellings. Leading questions can color how people respond. People are unaware of these effects and will often answer in an affirmative, confident, and convincing tone. Children seem especially prone to this type of memory distortion. The research is not clear on whether the original memory trace is affected by this type of reconstruction or not. **(Memory construction)**

Grade Yourself

Circle the numbers of the questions you missed, then fill in the total incorrect for each topic. If you answered more than three questions incorrectly, you need to focus on that topic. (If a topic has less than three questions and you had at least one wrong, we suggest you study that topic also. Read your textbook, a review book, or ask your teacher for help.)

Subject: Memory

Topic	Question Numbers	Number Incorrect
Memory types	1, 2, 4, 5, 6	
Encoding	3	
Chunking	7	
Rehearsal	8	
Serial position effect	9, 10	
Recall vs. recognition	11	
Retrieval cues	12	
Fogetting	13, 14	
Mood and memory	15	
Flashbulb memories	16	
Memory improvement	17, 19	
Memory construction	18, 20	

Thinking

Brief Yourself

Thinking is a cognitive process directed to understanding the world we live in. In broad terms, thinking is the application of human reason to solve "problems." Problem solving is behavior-directed toward achieving a goal. Reasoning is either deductive or inductive and often involves the application of schemas to particular types of problems. Algorithms and heuristics are two categories of procedures people employ to solve problems. Heuristic thinking is open to biases that may lead to incorrect answers. One of the hallmarks that distinguishes an expert from a novice is that he or she has many more schemas to guide his or her problem solving. Creative problem solvers are able to generate novel solutions not constrained by convention or traditional approaches. More recently, computer models have been constructed to simulate human thought as an aid to our understanding.

Test Yourself

1. Discuss the basic characteristics of thinking.

2. What are the different types, or modes, of thought?

3. What are the steps employed in problem solving?

4. What is functional fixedness?

5. Contrast algorithms and heuristics as problem-solving strategies.

6. What is the difference between deductive and inductive reasoning?

7. What are the representativeness heuristic and availability heuristic?

8. Describe the gambler's fallacy.

9. In terms of thinking strategies, what are some differences between experts and novices?

10. Describe the means/end analysis heuristic.

11. What are some characteristics of creative problem solvers?

12. What role do concepts play in thinking?

13. What is the relationship between concepts and language?

14. In terms of concepts, what are prototypes and natural categories?

15. In computer models of human thought, what is the difference between parallel and serial processing?

16. Discuss the "mind as computer" metaphor.

17. What is the relationship between incubation and insight?

18. What is "reasoning by analogy"?

19. What is the belief bias, and how can it affect our thinking?

20. Give an example of problem solving using imagery.

✔ Check Yourself

1. Thinking is abstract, symbolic, and relational. It is abstract in that the objects we reason about or with subsume all of the concrete, particular instances that are the focus of our thinking. It is symbolic because we often use words, numbers, and images to represent the things we are thinking of. It is relational because as a form of problem solving we attempt to proceed from the present state to the desired goal state, the "solution" to the problem. **(Definition)**

2. Propositional thought takes the form of verbal sentences that we can "hear" in our mind; it expresses a proposition or statement. Imaginal thought consists of images, particularly visual ones, that we can "see" in our mind. Motoric thought has also been proposed and is a mode of thought that relates mental representations to motor movements. **(Definition)**

3. Although there are many approaches or systems to this, one might be: (1) first, identify the problem; (2) next, frame the problem. What context does the problem occur in? What is the important and relevant information? What is the goal of your solution? (3) then explore and act on appropriate strategies and evaluate the obtained solutions; (4) finally, reevaluate your activities and solutions. Did you achieve your goals? **(Problem solving)**

4. Functional fixedness is a tendency to limit solutions to conventional or traditional answers. It is when the mind is blind to perceiving or understanding the components of a problem as anything other than their proper or intended function. **(Problem solving)**

5. An algorithm is a step-by-step procedure guaranteed to lead to the correct solution. A heuristic is a rule of thumb, a mental shortcut, that often leads to correct solutions but is not guaranteed to do so. Algorithms properly applied always work, but they can be time-consuming and laborious to use. Heuristics are general strategies that we learn to apply to particular situations; they are general guidelines about possible solutions. **(Problem solving)**

6. Both deduction and induction are forms of logical reasoning. In philosophic terms, logic is the art of non-contradictory identification, which means progressing from problem to solution such that all steps are true and no falsehoods or contradictions exist in the solution. Deductive reasoning progresses from general principles to a conclusion about a particular case. A conclusion cannot be false if the premises are true. Inductive reasoning works in the opposite direction, starting with specific facts to develop a general principle, for example, a medical diagnosis based on the patient's symptoms. Induction can lead to wrong conclusions when the specific facts are falsely or overly generalized using, for example, the availability heuristic. **(Reasoning)**

7. The representativeness and availability heuristics underlie much of our inductive decision-making. We use the representativeness heuristic to evaluate how similar something is to our prototype for a concept. The more similar it is, the more likely we will consider it as belonging to that concept. With the availability heuristic, we base decisions upon how readily available information is in memory. If similar instances come to mind easily or are plentiful, we may classify them as belonging to that category. Whereas the availability heuristic can lead to a belief bias or confirmation bias, people may confuse representativeness and probability when they use the representative heuristic. **(Problems with decision-making)**

8. The gambler's fallacy is a misuse of the statistical principle that independent events have no effect on prior or subsequent events. A fair coin tossed is equally likely to show heads or tails. Each toss of the coin is independent of all others and has no effect on which side lands showing. The coin has no "memory" of the prior tosses. To presume otherwise would mean that the act of tossing would have to physically alter the coin such that it was no longer fair and could thus bias the outcome. **(Problems with decision-making)**

9. Experts and novices differ in many ways, not the least of which is how much they know about a subject. In terms of thinking strategies, experts have many more schemas to bring to bear on a problem to guide their problem solving. Experts are also better able to recognize when each schema should be applied. Research reveals that when describing a problem, experts state it in terms of the underlying abstract principle, while novices focus on surface features of the problem. Experts also organize and chunk their knowledge in terms of principles rather than surface features. **(Expertise)**

10. Means/end analysis is a general problem-solving heuristic. The strategy involves identifying the differences between the present state and the desired goal or end state, and then acting so as to reduce these differences. Subgoal analysis is often employed in conjunction with means/end analysis. Subgoal analysis is breaking down a large or complex problem into subgoals that are intermediate to the final solution and more easily solved. **(Problem solving)**

11. Creative problem solvers are able to engage in divergent thinking, to generate novel ideas or variations on ideas that diverge from convention or tradition. Creative problem solvers also frame the problem in terms of principles rather than specific fact patterns. This leads them to generate more potential ideas as solutions. In a particular field, the more knowledge someone has, the more creative their solutions will likely be because they have organized their knowledge in terms of the principles. They will also be better equipped to evaluate their ideas, to engage in convergent thinking to narrow the alternatives and select the best one. **(Creativity)**

12. Concepts are mental abstractions that serve to unite events, people, or things that share some common feature(s). The most important role concepts play is to reduce the number of units our mind must deal with. (Recall "the magical number 7, plus or minus 2.") Concepts represent condensations of knowledge and are the basic units of thinking. When recalling a concept, we often think of a prototype or best example of the category, but the concept proper is an artifact of the human mind and should not be confused with the prototype. **(Concepts)**

13. Language is a conceptual tool, a code of visual-auditory symbols that denote concepts. They provide a system of cognitive classification and organization. Although there is some disagreement on this point, concepts and language are primarily a tool of cognition; communication, although crucial, is secondary because cognition must precede any attempt at communicating. **(Concepts)**

14. A prototype is a representative sample of a class of things, a best example that represents most of the "family resemblances." Prototypes are abstractions of many features, some perceptual, others not, some of which might represent an ideal that has no exact match in reality. Natural categories or concepts are simple, encountered often, familiar, and easily characterized by prototypes. These are termed "natural" because they seem to represent basic categories of things such as living versus nonliving. **(Concepts)**

15. Parallel processing is the ability to carry out many different activities at once. In terms of problem solving it means working on different aspects of the problem simultaneously. This is what most human thought is believed to be. Serial processing means processing sequentially, that the "input" of one stage cannot begin until the "output" of the prior stage has been completed. **(Problem solving)**

16. Although no one believes that computer circuits are anything at all like human brains, adherents of the metaphor believe that by "teaching" a computer to solve problems we will expand our understanding of human thinking. The scientific value lies in stimulating new ideas and fostering insight. Critics argue that even the most sophisticated computer does not approach the complexity of the human mind and thus cannot adequately model what cognition is. But models do not have to be complete or correct to be scientifically useful. (**Computer analogies**)

17. Insight is a sudden and distinctive reconceptualization of the problem or the sudden comprehension of a new idea. Insight usually follows a period of incubation, a period of time following intense study when the problem is temporarily set aside. The problem is said to be "incubating" at a subconscious level. Insight is sometimes called the "Aha!" effect. (**Insight**)

18. Reasoning by analogy is transferring the underlying principle of the problem's solution to a new problem. Although the new problem is superficially different, the principle underlying the solution—the structure of the solution—is the same. The two problems are said to be isomorphic. People have difficulty transferring solutions from one problem to another, often doing so on the basis of content instead of the relationship among the elements of the problem. (**Reasoning**)

19. Belief bias is the tendency to accept as logical those conclusions that agree with our opinions. Related to this is belief perseverance, our tendency to cling to beliefs even in the face of contrary evidence. Both forms of illogical reasoning ignore evidence that undermines the belief. (**Problems with decision-making**)

20. Much of human problem solving takes propositional form, although for some tasks visualization is faster and more efficient. For example, when asked whether a kangaroo's back legs are shorter than its front legs, the part of the brain where visualization is carried out becomes more active. In mental rotation experiments where subjects have to decide which views of an object as seen from different orientations are the same, the time required to judge is a function of how many degrees the figures must be rotated. (**Problem solving**)

Grade Yourself

Circle the numbers of the questions you missed, then fill in the total incorrect for each topic. If you answered more than three questions incorrectly, you need to focus on that topic. (If a topic has less than three questions and you had at least one wrong, we suggest you study that topic also. Read your textbook, a review book, or ask your teacher for help.)

Subject: Thinking

Topic	Question Numbers	Number Incorrect
Definition	1, 2	
Problem solving	3, 4, 5, 10, 15, 20	
Reasoning	6, 18	
Problems with decision-making	7, 8, 19	
Expertise	9	
Creativity	11	
Concepts	12, 13, 14	
Computer analogies	16	
Insight	17	

Language

10

Brief Yourself

Language is a conceptual tool, a code of visual-auditory symbols that denote concepts. Concepts and language provide a system — a method — of cognitive classification and organization. The two most-important roles language plays in human thought is as a tool of cognition and as a means of communication. Human language is symbolic, structured, and generative. Linguistics is the study of language and its rules. Language has both a surface structure and a deep structure. The surface structure consists of the way symbols are combined within a language, and the deep structure refers to the underlying meaning of the combined symbols. One of the most-striking child development changes is the transition from uttering seemingly meaningless sounds to using a complex language. Recent research reveals that congenitally deaf children raised by deaf parents and taught American Sign Language (ASL) from birth use signs in thinking and dreaming much the same way hearing children use sounds or spoken words.

Test Yourself

1. Explain what "symbolic," "structured," and "generative" mean in terms of language.

2. Define syntax and semantics.

3. What are phonemes and morphemes?

4. What happens during the babbling stage of language development?

5. Noam Chomsky argued that humans possess a language acquisition device (LAD). What is it?

6. What is "universal grammar"?

7. What is the difference between a word-order syntax and a word-ending syntax?

8. Does the age at which a person learns a second language matter in terms of how well he or she masters it?

9. What do proponents of Whorf's linguistic relativity hypothesis contend?

10. What is "motherese"?

11. At what age does telegraphic speech begin, and what does it indicate?

12. As to communication, what factors affect how meaning is constructed in the mind?

13. What role does context play in language?

14. Will expanding your vocabulary affect how you think?

15. What is the difference between communication and language?

16. What is a "slip of the tongue?

17. Give some examples of human nonverbal communication.

18. What might be some advantages of an auditory compared to a visual (gestural) language?

19. Do animals use language?

20. Discuss nonhuman communication.

✔ Check Yourself

1. Language is symbolic because it uses sounds, signs (writings), and gestures to represent objects and ideas. It is structured in that rules govern how symbols may be combined to create meaningful units. It is generative because symbols can be combined in an infinite number of ways to create messages, each with novel meaning. **(Definition)**

2. Syntax are the rules for combining the symbols in a language; they are part of a language's surface structure. Semantics are the rules for connecting the symbols to their referents, to their meanings. Where syntax prescribes how the various types of words (e.g., noun, verb, adjective) are assembled to produce a sentence, semantics governs how meaning is derived from the assembled words — either to produce the sentence or later interpret it. **(Definition)**

3. Phonemes are the smallest units of sound in a language, the building blocks of speech. English uses about 40 phonemes; although humans are capable of producing about 100 phonemes, no language uses all of them. Phonemes are combined into morphemes, which are the smallest units of meaning in a language. For example, *dog* is one morpheme, while *dog/s* is two because the added *s* denotes multiple individuals. Phonemes, the smallest unit of sound in a language, are combined to form morphemes, the smallest unit of meaning in a language. Morphemes are combined to form words, words into phrases, and phrases into sentences. **(Definition)**

4. At about four months of age, babies make a variety of sounds—sounds found in a variety of human languages from around the world. When babbling begins, it is not possible to tell what language a child is exposed to in daily life. By about ten months of age, sounds other than those in the native tongue are no longer uttered. Deaf babies babble, thus babbling is not an imitation of adult speech. **(Language development)**

5. Chomsky believed that all humans are born with some knowledge about the structural properties of language, something like a genetic blueprint for the underlying aspects of language. He called this a language acquisition device (LAD) and argued that it also possessed a set of cognitive and perceptual abilities specialized for language learning. Other linguists believe instead that language development is a consequence of the developing brain and not some innate structure. **(Chomsky)**

6. Universal grammar is an aspect of Chomsky's LAD that provides the rules, conditions, and principles for understanding and producing language. Universal grammar is posited to be similar in all languages, whether verbal or nonverbal. **(Chomsky)**

7. Many languages, including English, have a word-order syntax, which means the order of words conveys meaning. For example, the sentence "The girl threw the ball" has a very different meaning than "The ball threw the girl." Other languages, such as German, employ a word-ending syntax in which the order of the words is variable. The suffix attached to the words conveys who the actors are and what they are acting on. Children who learn a language with a word-ending syntax learn that word order is not important, but that word endings are. **(Language commonalities)**

8. Yes. Young children exposed to a second language early in life could master it about as well as their first language. After the age of three to seven, though, mastery progressively declines, especially in terms of grammar. A second language can certainly be learned after this age, but the fluency will be less than with the first language. (**Language learning**)

9. Benjamin Whorf contended that language not only influences but determines how and what we think. For example, Eskimos have many words for snow while most of us have only one word. Whorf concluded that Eskimos actually perceive "snow" differently from the rest of us. More recent research has demonstrated that this view, at least in its extreme, is false. Researchers today would instead agree that language reflects basic aspects of human perception and thought that can influence how we categorize our experience. (**Whorf**)

10. Motherese is a child-directed speech used by parents in all cultures: high-pitched intonations to attract their children's attention, falling intonations to comfort them, and staccato bursts for prohibitions. The sentences are short, less complex, with more repetition, and pronounced with better articulation. Pet owners often speak to their pets in a similar way. (**Motherese**)

11. Telegraphic speech begins at about eighteen months of age and consists of the child's first multiword utterances, typically two or three words in length. They contain only the essential elements, such as "more cookie," leaving out unessential words. This type of speech signals the beginning of multiword grammar. (**Language development**)

12. The symbols we communicate with do not have any inherent meaning. One aspect of language is the association of a particular meaning with a symbol — a word or phrase. We communicate by exchanging symbols and transforming the symbols; therefore, meaning is constructed in the mind; thus, it is a product of cognition. Our knowledge, expectations, and the situational context determine the specific meaning we derive from the symbols. If an expert chess player and a novice one are shown the same game board, they will each derive a different meaning from it; while the novice may see only the position of the various pieces, an expert may also see the earlier progression of the game that led to the present board. Our expectations can differ depending on where we are or with whom we are communicating. Both knowledge and expectations are part of the broader issue of context; not only must each person associate a similar meaning with a symbol; but he or she must apply it in a given situation. (**Communication**)

13. Context greatly affects how we understand language. It aids comprehension because people base conversations on shared topics and understanding of a listener's point of view. When participants do not share the same referential information, communication breaks down. A new person joining an ongoing conversation often cannot immediately understand what is being discussed; he or she must first listen to a series of interchanges to build up a sense of meaning. A simple example might be the meaning of an acronym; STP means standard temperature and pressure to a chemist, but an engine oil additive to an automobile mechanic. (**Communication**)

14. Yes. Recall that language and the concepts it denotes are a system for cognitive classification and organization. Your vocabulary reflects not only the content of your mind, but also how it is organized. The new concepts you learn studying psychology will influence how you think about behavior. Similarly with children, they become capable of thinking in more-sophisticated ways as their vocabulary expands. (**Communication**)

15. Communication is a broader concept than language. Whereas language has a number of requirements (see answer #1 above), communication boils down to a sender sending a message to a receiver. An element of intentionality is usually required such that the sender intends to send a message to a receiver. Further,

while communication can occur at all levels of complexity, language is, by its nature, highly complex. **(Communication)**

16. A slip of the tongue is an inadvertent semantic or articulatory mistake in what we say. One interpretation is that we have a language of thought that differs from the language though which we express our thoughts. Slips of the tongue may provide insight into how people use language and how they think. Thus they may help us gain a better understanding of normal language processing. **(Slips of the tongue)**

17. Human nonverbal communication consists of two main parts, prosody and paralanguage. Prosody is that aspect of language that includes rhythm, loudness, and tempo. Paralanguage is subdivided into vocal and nonverbal aspects. Vocal paralanguage includes such things as a laugh, a cry, a groan, or a nonword sound intended to amplify or clarify the meaning of the spoken word. Nonverbal paralanguage is what most people think of when referring to nonverbal communication and includes body language, facial expressions, gestures, and the like. Nonverbal paralanguage supplements meaning. **(Nonverbal communication)**

18. Some advantages of an auditory language compared to a visual (gestural) one include that it works in the dark, line of sight is not necessary, it works at a distance, and the number of possible signals is likely greater. **(Language comparisons)**

19. Research has shown that apes have a limited ability to acquire some elements of language using American Sign Language or plastic symbols and chips that represent "words." Animal language is very concrete and relates primarily to physical objects and needs. Animals are not able to communicate abstract ideas or master complex grammar. Their language abilities are dwarfed by the typical four-year-old child. **(Animal language)**

20. Many animals communicate with other members of their own species. The dancing pattern of bees in a hive can indicate the location of food. Whales, dolphins, and monkeys use specific sounds to indicate approaching danger. The gestures and odors of dogs signal sexual and aggressive readiness. Moths broadcast a chemical signal to attract a mate. Most psychologists do not consider animal communication "language" because it is not symbolic. **(Animal language)**

Grade Yourself

Circle the numbers of the questions you missed, then fill in the total incorrect for each topic. If you answered more than three questions incorrectly, you need to focus on that topic. (If a topic has less than three questions and you had at least one wrong, we suggest you study that topic also. Read your textbook, a review book, or ask your teacher for help.)

Subject: Language

Topic	Question Numbers	Number Incorrect
Definition	1, 2, 3	
Language development	4, 11	
Chomsky	5, 6	
Language commonalities	7	
Language learning	8	
Whorf	9	
Motherese	10	
Communication	12, 13, 14, 15	
Slips of the tongue	16	
Nonverbal communication	17	
Language comparisons	18	
Animal language	19, 20	

Intelligence

Brief Yourself

Intelligence is the ability to grasp the facts of reality. This comprises acquiring knowledge, thinking and reasoning effectively, and dealing adaptively with the environment. Spearman conceptualized intelligence as consisting of two elements, a general ("g") factor that was the core of intelligence, along with specific cognitive abilities. Thurstone viewed intelligence as a set of specific abilities — primary mental abilities (e.g., verbal, visual-spatial) — rather than any underlying general factor. Both of these positions view intelligence as a form of mental competence. The theory of multiple intelligences diverges from this in that there are instead distinct varieties of intelligence, each of which is adaptive within its own environment (e.g., linguistic, musical, bodily-kinesthetic). The particular level of intelligence a person has is determined by both genetic and environmental factors, but the use of intelligence is an acquired skill.

Test Yourself

1. What two assumptions did Binet make pertaining to intelligence, and why are they relevant for intelligence testing?

2. What is "mental age"? Is this concept popular today?

3. How do the Wechsler tests of intelligence differ from the Stanford-Binet variety?

4. What is the difference between achievement and aptitude tests?

5. Define the term "predictive validity" and apply it to intelligence tests.

6. Contrast the psychometric and cognitive psychology approaches to intelligence.

7. What are Thurstone's "factors of the mind"?

8. Contrast crystallized and fluid intelligence.

9. What components make up Gardner's theory of multiple intelligences?

10. What is heritability? How does it apply to intelligence?

11. How have twin and sibling studies contributed to our understanding of the heritability of intelligence?

12. Can a child raised in an environmentally deprived environment be as intelligent as a child raised in an enriched one?

13. Are there gender differences in intelligence? Give examples to support your position.

14. Are there differences in intelligence attributable to race?

15. What is "mainstreaming"?

16. Are "gifted" children eccentric and socially maladjusted? What are they like as adults?

17. Are enrichment programs equally effective at all periods in a child's life?

18. What is the relationship between giftedness and creativity?

19. What is standardization, and how does it apply to psychological tests?

20. What is test reliability?

21. What is test validity? Describe the difference between content and predictive validity.

Check Yourself

1. Alfred Binet made two assumptions about intelligence: (1) mental abilities develop over time; and (2) that the rate at which people gain mental competence is fairly constant over time. So adults should be more intelligent or mentally competent than children, just as an older child should be more competent than a younger child. And a child more competent at age twelve was also likely more competent at age six. To gauge intelligence fairly, therefore, the testing tasks must be age-dependent, with a twelve-year-old expected to do more than a six-year-old for an equivalent rating on the measurement scale. **(Intelligence tests)**

2. Mental age was the score reflecting a child's mental development. Binet identified the types of problems children of different ages should be able to do, and based on their performance they were assigned a mental age indicating the level of mental competence they had attained. This concept was later expanded to include the ratio of mental age to chronological age and called an intelligence quotient (IQ). Today mental age is no longer used. Instead of specific tasks serving as the gauge, a child is compared to other same-age children's performance, a population norm. The resultant IQ is computed relative to this population norm, not performance on specific tasks, as was the original mental age. **(Intelligence tests)**

3. The Stanford-Binet test focuses on verbal tasks. David Wechsler believed verbal skills were only one aspect of intelligence, that there were nonverbal abilities the Stanford-Binet did not assess. The Wechsler tests include two classes of subtests, Verbal Tests (e.g., comprehension, digit span) and Performance Tests (e.g., picture completion, object assembly). While each class of subtests yielded its own IQ, they could be reported together as a Full-Scale IQ. **(Intelligence tests)**

4. An achievement test is a direct measure of what someone has learned or can do: it depends heavily on prior learning. An aptitude test attempts to assess the potential for future learning and performance by presenting new, puzzle-like problems; the claim is that this type of test depends less on prior learning. **(Intelligence tests)**

5. Predictive validity is a measure of how well performance in one situation predicts performance in a different situation. For example, the SAT college selection test is used to select applicants because it does a relatively good job of predicting grade-point averages. In this example, GPA is the criterion, and the SAT score is used to predict GPA. High predictability means high predictive validity. **(Measuring intelligence)**

6. Each of these two approaches attempts to understand the factors that comprise intelligence. The psychometric approach attempts to specify the structure of intelligence, while the cognitive psychology approach focuses on why there are individual differences. Identifying how many classes of mental ability there are belongs to the psychometric approach. Why people differ in each of these abilities and what factors affect development and performance are the purview of the cognitive psychology approach. **(Measuring intelligence)**

7. Thurstone believed that human mental performance depended on seven distinct abilities, "primary mental abilities" or "factors of the mind." The abilities included space, verbal comprehension, word fluency, number facility, perceptual speed, rote memory, and reasoning. He noted that people's performance on different mental tasks correlated less than perfectly. He did not believe that Spearman's "g" factor was sufficient to account for this discrepancy, and this was the explanation he offered instead. **(Nature of intelligence)**

8. More contemporary researchers have broken down Spearman's general intelligence into two correlated but not identical abilities: crystallized intelligence and fluid intelligence. Crystallized intelligence is the ability to understand relationships, make judgments, and solve problems, or, from a different perspective, to apply previously learned knowledge to current problems. Fluid intelligence is the general ability to perceive, encode, and reason about information, to deal with novel problem-solving situations. Fluid intelligence is used to establish crystallized intelligence, and over the adult years performance on tests of fluid intelligence declines, while performance on tests of crystallized intelligence improves. (**Nature of intelligence**)

9. Gardner's theory of multiple intelligences includes six distinct types of intelligences: linguistic, mathematical, visual-spatial, musical, bodily-kinesthetic, and personal. The latter three are not measured by any existing tests. Gardner proposed this theory to account for individuals with seemingly special gifts (e.g., Mozart), savants, and patterns of behavior of those with brain damage. (**Nature of intelligence**)

10. Heritability is the proportion of variability in a trait that is attributable to genetic factors. Applied to intelligence, it means that only 50 percent to 70 percent of the variance in intelligence scores in the U.S. population is attributable to the genetic makeup of a person. Heritability refers only to variations within a group. It cannot be used to compare two different groups such as the United States and India, or even different socioeconomic groups in the U.S. (**Nature of intelligence**)

11. The correlation of IQ scores between identical twins raised together is .86; raised apart, .75; siblings raised together, .45; and raised apart, .21. Clearly there is a genetic component, but because there is a difference in whether they are raised together or apart, something more than genetics is at work. That variation within each group attributable to genetics is the heritability of intelligence. Other factors affecting IQ are the environment and interactions between genes and the environment. (**Genetics**)

12. Yes. Many researchers believe that intelligence is malleable, that it can be shaped and even "taught." Underlying this view is the concept of a reaction range, the genetically determined upper and lower bounds for a trait. Differences in the environment will then determine to what extent the genetic endowment is actualized. Children raised in an enriched environment will tend to come out nearer the upper bound of their reaction range, while those raised in a deprived one will fall nearer the lower bound. Thus actualized intelligence is the result of genetic-environmental interactions and how we choose to take advantage of opportunities the environment provides. (**Environment**)

13. It would be wrong to say that there are differences in intelligence between men and women. Some specific differences in cognitive abilities have been reported in the literature, but they are slight, average differences only. Several physical characteristics of the brain also vary between men and women. Environmental factors such as sex-typed activities, have also been posited as to why the skill levels are different. For instance, men tend to outperform women on certain spatial tasks and mathematical reasoning, while women tend to perform better on verbal fluency and mathematical calculation. (**Gender differences**)

14. This is a hotly debated issue. That races may differ in performance on intelligence tests is not disputed, while the cause of the difference is. Races within a country can vary just as countries can vary in how well the population as a whole performs. In any event, most studies find that the tests are an accurate predictor of performance on the criterion task, regardless of race. The conclusion is that the tests seem to tap the cognitive skills utilized by the construct intelligence. (**Genetics**)

15. Mainstreaming is the practice of placing cognitively disabled children in the regular classroom instead of in special education classes. This accelerates the disabled child's social skill and academic development, while minimizing the stigma associated with being labeled "retarded." (**Extremes of intelligence**)

16. No. A study of gifted children by Lewis Terman, beginning in 1921 and extending over the next sixty years, reported that they had high levels of adjustment in both adolescence and adulthood, their marriages tended to be happy and successful, and in addition had numerous accomplishments in their professional lives. **(Extremes of intelligence)**

17. Both enriched and deprived environments are capable of influencing intellectual growth. Enrichment programs are most effective when carried out early in a child's life. If a child remains in a very deprived environment, later enrichment programs will have less effect. **(Environment)**

18. IQ score is a poor predictor of who will win awards for accomplishments in a field. Thus, among gifted individuals, IQ score is a poor predictor of success. Creativity is often associated with divergent thinking, the generation of novel answers and solutions that diverge from the norm. Knowledge and experience are still prerequisites, but there is a growing body of research that suggests that motivation and personality also contribute to creativity. An average-to-above-average IQ contributes to creativity, but beyond this the constructs are relatively separate. **(Creativity)**

19. Standardization allows a meaningful comparison between a person's score on an intelligence test and the scores from a pretested, representative sample of people. Standardized test results usually form a normal, or bell-shaped curve. **(Intelligence tests)**

20. Test reliability is determined by having people take the very same test again (or some form of it.) If the two scores are consistent and about the same, it is reliable. **(Intelligence tests)**

21. Validity is the degree to which the test measures what it was designed to measure, or predicts what it was supposed to. Content validity means that the test addresses what it should, whereas predictive validity shows what future performance will be like. **(Intelligence tests)**

Grade Yourself

Circle the numbers of the questions you missed, then fill in the total incorrect for each topic. If you answered more than three questions incorrectly, you need to focus on that topic. (If a topic has less than three questions and you had at least one wrong, we suggest you study that topic also. Read your textbook, a review book, or ask your teacher for help.)

Subject: Intelligence

Topic	Question Numbers	Number Incorrect
Intelligence tests	1, 2, 3, 19, 20, 21	
Measuring intelligence	4, 5, 6	
Nature of intelligence	7, 8, 9, 10	
Genetics	11, 14	
Environment	12, 17	
Gender differences	13	
Extremes of intelligence	15, 16	
Creativity	18	

Consciousness

12

Brief Yourself

Consciousness is the faculty of awareness, the faculty of perceiving that which exists. It refers to our moment-to-moment awareness of ourselves and our environment and provides us with a stable personal identity. Consciousness is a private event so it cannot be observed directly; instead, it must be studied using externally observable and measurable responses. Awareness is not a passive state, but an active one. While the chapters on sensation and perception emphasize the neurological factors leading to awareness, the present chapter focuses on the higher (conceptual) levels, including awareness itself, sleep, dreaming, hypnosis, and drug-induced altered states of consciousness.

Test Yourself

1. What techniques are used to study consciousness?

2. What is the difference between automatic and controlled processing?

3. Describe the differences among the four mental states used to describe our awareness.

4. What effect does practice have on mental processing?

5. What is the "module" view of mind?

6. What is the circadian rhythm?

7. What is an EEG, and what is it used for?

8. Describe the stages of sleep.

9. Why do we sleep?

10. What are some reasons proposed to explain why we dream?

11. Provide brief definitions for the following sleep disorders: insomnia, hypersomnia, and sleep apnea.

12. What was Freud's explanation for why we dream? Distinguish between manifest content and latent content.

13. When does REM rebound occur?

14. What is the phenomenon of "lucid dreaming"?

15. Does mediation produce a dramatically altered state of consciousness? Explain.

16. What is hypnosis?

17. Does hypnosis improve memory?

18. Can hypnosis be used to treat pain?

19. By what mechanism do psychoactive drugs affect consciousness?

20. What effect does alcohol have on the nervous system?

21. What are psychotomimetic drugs?

22. What are stimulants? Give examples.

 # Check Yourself

1. Because consciousness cannot be observed directly, externally observable responses must be used to infer its nature. Three classes of technique are commonly employed: physiological responses (e.g., brain waves); verbal self-reports of inner experiences; and nonverbal behaviors such as reading, looking in a mirror, and so on. (**Research methods**)

2. Cognitive psychologists distinguish between mental processes that are effortful and demanding of attention and those that seem to occur effortlessly. The former is controlled processing and is further characterized by being easily interrupted and relatively slow. The latter is automatic processing and occurs rapidly without conscious attention; examples include perceptual schemas to interpret stimuli, and reading. (**Mental processes**)

3. The four states used to describe our awareness are conscious, subconscious, preconscious, and unconscious. Conscious events are internal or external stimuli in our immediate awareness. Subconscious awareness refers to stimuli that are being processed automatically and that can be brought into conscious awareness if we focus our attention on it—for example, the position of our limbs as we walk. Preconscious events are those not in awareness at the moment but which can be easily brought to mind, such as the name of a pet. Unconscious material cannot be brought to mind easily or possibly at all, such as a memory of a painful childhood experience. The term "nonconscious" is sometimes used to describe those things that cannot be brought into awareness, such as the workings of the rods and cones in our eyes or the pattern recognition mechanism of audition. (**Types of awareness**)

4. Practice automatizes a mental event or series of events. Through practice that which starts as slow, effortful, controlled processing becomes rapid, effortless, and automatic. Learning to walk or drive took tremendous concentration in the beginning, and today we often do them while also doing two or three other things simultaneously. (**Practice**)

5. Although the mind has been viewed as having different functions such as memory and perception, it has always been seen as a single, unified entity. The "module" model of mind posits that the mind is composed of information-processing units that each perform simple and specific tasks. The modules operate largely independently, can be arranged hierarchically, and operate at an unconscious level. Some modules might process a specific type of sensory input, while others might integrate the outputs of other modules before the contents ascend to conscious awareness. (**Theories of mind**)

6. The circadian rhythm is the biologically based twenty-four-hour activity cycle that governs the energy level of humans, other species and plants. It is a biological rhythm that involves daily cyclical changes in body temperature, blood pressure, hormonal secretions, and other bodily processes. We normally sleep at the low point of the daily temperature cycle. (**Sleep**)

7. An electroencephalogram (EEG) is a record of the brain's electrical activities as measured by an instrument called an electroencephalograph. It is used to measure the stages of sleep. Prior to the invention of the electroencephalograph sleep, was thought to be a single state. (**Research methods**)

8. The brain wave patterns recorded on an EEG are how the first four stages of sleep are distinguished. Alpha waves (8–12 cycles per second) characterize a relaxed waking state. Stage 1 sleep is a light sleep and consists of theta waves (3–7 cps). Stage 2 sleep (12–14 cps) is characterized by occasional sleep spindles and K complexes. Stage 3 sleep is a deeper sleep with occasional delta waves (0.5–2 cps). Delta waves are large, slow waves that indicate a synchronized pattern of brain cell firings. In Stage 4 sleep, the delta waves predominate. The fifth stage of sleep is called REM sleep because of the characteristic rapid eye movements that occur every half-minute or so. This stage has also been called dream sleep because we do most of our dreaming in this stage. The EEG activity shows brain waves that are closer to our normal waking pattern, which indicates a high level of general cortical arousal. (**Sleep**)

9. No firm answer yet exists for this question. One answer that has been suggested is that since night was a dangerous time for our ancestors because of predators, creatures that stayed quiet at night had a better chance of surviving. A biological function has also been suggested, to maintain homeostasis. Although a restorative function involving regeneration of important brain chemicals has also been proposed, no specific neurotransmitters have been identified. (**Sleep**)

10. One function proposed for why we dream is for memory consolidation, to reorganize information learned during the day. The opposite view has also been put forth—that dreaming enhances mental functioning by helping us to forget, a way for the brain to purge itself of unwanted or unimportant content that might interfere with significant material. (**Dreams**)

11. Insomnia is a class of sleep disorders characterized by abnormal wakefulness. It may be associated with an altered work cycle, alcohol and drug abuse, emotional problems, and so on. Hypersomnia is uncontrollable sleepiness. Narcolepsy is a condition that involves irresistible sleep attacks, and sufferers often go directly from being wide awake to REM sleep, skipping the other sleep stages. Sleep apnea is characterized by a difficulty in breathing while asleep, with breathing often stopping as often as 500 times per night before the sleeper wakes up with a loud snore of taking in air. (**Sleep disorders**)

12. Freud believed dreaming to be an expression of repressed wishes and that the aim of any dream was wish fulfillment. The manifest content is the person's report of a dream and served to hide or disguise the real psychological meaning of the dream, its latent content. Freud believed the latent content of most dreams revolved around sex and aggression. (**Dreams**)

13. REM rebound occurs when someone is deprived of REM sleep. When the person is allowed to sleep uninterrupted, a REM–deprived individual spends about 50 percent more time in REM sleep than normal. (**Sleep**)

14. Lucid dreaming is the experience of dreaming and being fully aware that you are dreaming. While in this state, the lucid dreamer is unable to perceive any sensory information from the real world; he or she is aware only of his or her dream world. The lucid dreamer is often able to consciously control the content of the dream. This phenomenon is relatively rare and has only just begun to be studied. (**Dreams**)

15. There are few reports of people experiencing a dramatically altered state of consciousness such as we associate with drugs. Meditation produces a general "relaxation response" that can be further distinguished as somatic or cognitive. Other techniques such as exercise or restful reading are as effective

as meditation in producing somatic (bodily) relaxation. Meditation is seen as particularly effective for inducing cognitive (mental) relaxation because it diverts attention from intrusive and anxiety-arousing thoughts. (**Meditation**)

16. No clear or agreed-upon definition of hypnosis exists. Hypnosis is not sleep. No unique physiological properties have been identified that would enable us to tell who is hypnotized and who is not, including EEG patterns. It has been described as a state of heightened suggestibility in which people seem to enter a trancelike state. Others argue that it is more like a very effective form of communication between hypnotist and subject. A role-playing theory has also been proposed—that hypnotized people behave according to their preconceived notions and expectations, and use these to guide their behavior. People cannot be hypnotized against their will, nor can they be induced to commit an act they would not otherwise commit while in a normal waking state. (In Stanley Milgram's obedience experiments, subjects in a normal waking state complied with the experimenter's instructions to give people electric shocks.) (**Hypnosis**)

17. Research suggests that the improved recall often associated with hypnosis is more likely due to effective memory retrieval techniques than the hypnosis itself. Other research has found an increase in the overall rate of reporting with hypnosis, for both accurate and inaccurate information. One complication is that people under hypnosis are more confident in their judgments that what they recall is accurate, even when they are wrong. This has led many states to ban from courts of law hypnotically improved memory. (**Hypnosis**)

18. Hypnosis has been used to control pain during surgery since the nineteenth century. In the mid-1800s, James Esdaile performed more than 300 major surgeries using hypnosis as the sole anesthetic. This use continues today. Hypnosis is also used with children to relieve the pain associated with treatment for bone marrow transplant. The mechanism for how this works is unknown, but some researchers have suggested that hypnosis dissociates the physical perception of pain by blocking it from conscious awareness. (**Hypnosis**)

19. Psychoactive drugs are those that affect a person's psychological state. They produce their effects by altering the normal functioning of neurons. They produce their effects in five ways: (1) Psychoactive drugs can mimic a natural neurotransmitter and occupy a receptor site and cause the neuron to fire. (2) They can occupy a receptor site without causing the neuron to fire, thus preventing the neurotransmitter from reaching the neuron. (3) The drug can penetrate the neuron's membrane and prevent it from manufacturing neurotransmitter substances. (4) It can prevent the release of neurotransmitters into the synapse so the neuron's ability to transmit information is disabled. (5) The drug can prevent the re-uptake of a neurotransmitter so that it continues to stimulate other neurons, thus greatly increasing neural firing. The effect on a given individual is influenced by the dosage, frequency of use, the person's size and psychological state, types of food recently eaten, and so on. (**Drugs**)

20. Alcohol is a depressant. It is absorbed directly into the bloodstream through the walls of the stomach and small intestine and carried to the brain. It is a depressant because it reduces electrical impulses and increases the activity of GABA, a neurotransmitter that inhibits synaptic activity. The net effect is impaired memory functioning, slower mental processing, and reduced efficacy performing any complex task such as driving. The euphoric "high" people experience after light drinking is a depression of inhibitory control mechanisms in the cortex. (**Drugs**)

21. Psychotomimetic drugs are hallucinogens, or mind-altering drugs. In addition to the effect of the drug itself, the user's mood, mental attitude, and environment contribute to the overall experience. Hallucinations are characteristic of these drugs. They include drugs such as mescaline, peyote, and LSD. **(Drugs)**

22. Stimulants speed up the transmission of messages in the nervous system. Some examples are cocaine, amphetamines, and caffeine. **(Drugs)**

Grade Yourself

Circle the numbers of the questions you missed, then fill in the total incorrect for each topic. If you answered more than three questions incorrectly, you need to focus on that topic. (If a topic has less than three questions and you had at least one wrong, we suggest you study that topic also. Read your textbook, a review book, or ask your teacher for help.)

Subject: Consciousness

Topic	Question Numbers	Number Incorrect
Research methods	1, 7	
Mental processes	2	
Types of awareness	3	
Practice	4	
Theories of mind	5	
Sleep	6, 8, 9, 13	
Dreams	10, 12, 14	
Sleep disorders	11	
Meditation	15	
Hypnosis	16, 17, 18	
Drugs	19, 20, 21, 22	

Motivation and Emotion

13

Brief Yourself

Several theories have been put forth to explain why people become motivated. People are motivated to eat, have sex, and achieve goals in life, to name a few things. People also experience arousal and are motivated due to emotional influences. Psychologists have identified a broad range of emotions and have developed theories to attempt to explain how emotions operate.

Test Yourself

1. Abraham Maslow described a motivational hierarchy. What does the hierarchy explain, and what do the levels consist of?

2. What is homeostasis?

3. How is drive-reduction theory related to arousal theory?

4. How does body chemistry play a role in hunger? Give details.

5. What parts of the brain control eating behavior? How do they work?

6. What is a set point? Can it be changed? If so, how?

7. What research has been done to show how external incentives play a role in hunger?

8. Name and describe two eating disorders.

9. What are the stages of the sexual response cycle identified by Masters and Johnson?

10. How do external stimuli play a role in sexual interest in humans?

11. Define achievement motivation. Mention how intrinsic and extrinsic achievement are involved.

12. How does physiological arousal play a role in emotion? What are some of the physiological states that are seen in various emotions? Give examples.

13. Provide cross-cultural information on emotions.

14. How can emotions be expressed through nonverbal communication?

15. Contrast the James-Lange theory with the Cannon-Bard theory of emotion.

16. Describe Schachter's Theory of Emotion.

17. Explain how cognition plays a role in emotion.

18. What are some of the purposes of fear?

19. Summarize some of the research on happiness. What are some of the predictors of happiness?

20. Discuss the research on anger.

21. Describe the Adaptation–Level Principle as compared to the Relative Deprivation Principle.

✔ Check Yourself

1. Maslow's hierarchy is a hierarchy of *needs*. He proposed the hierarchy to explain how some needs take precedence over others. From the bottom (most basic) to the top of the hierarchy, the needs include: physiological, safety, belongingness/love, self-esteem, and self-actualization, For example, the physiological needs for food and shelter must be met before needs for love and needs for self-esteem can truly be met. **(Hierarchy of motives)**

2. Homeostasis is the maintenance of an unchanging internal state. Homeostasis means "staying the same." The body works, for example, to maintain a constant, internal body temperature by means of sweating and shivering. The process of homeostasis gets less efficient with age. **(Physiology of motivation)**

3. Drive reduction theory is based on the idea that a physiological need, such as the need for water, causes the body to be psychologically aroused to reduce the need, by seeking out water. Due to homeostasis, the body seeks to reduce the drives. Arousal theory discusses the idea that people engage in behaviors to increase their arousal. Although all biological needs seem to be met, the body will seek out stimulation of some type. Boredom leads to a search for arousal, but too much arousal and the resulting stress lead to a search for a way to decrease the amount of arousal. **(Theories of motivation)**

4. Stomach contractions play a role, but even people and animals without stomachs get hungry. Body chemistry plays a further role in the experience of hunger. The body keeps track of the amount of glucose, a simple sugar, in the blood. When the glucose level drops, a person feels hungry. Rising levels of the hormone insulin help cause glucose levels to drop. **(Physiology of motivation)**

5. The key parts of the brain that control hunger are the lateral and ventromedial hypothalamus. The hypothalamus monitors the levels of glucose and insulin, in order to keep them in balance. The lateral hypothalamus (LH), when stimulated with electricity, will cause a sated rat to eat. Similarly, when stimulated with electricity, the ventromedial hypothalamus (VMH) will stop eating behavior, even in a starving rat. Lesioning, or destroying, the areas causes the opposite behavioral reactions. **(Physiology of motivation)**

6. A set point is the body's tendency to stay at a particular weight that is genetically determined. The set point can be lowered by means of regular aerobic exercise. However, some researchers think that hunger is more complex, due to learning, and that there is no such thing as a precise set point. **(Physiology of motivation)**

7. Judith Rodin conducted work on external incentives as they relate to hunger. She identified people who, when full, were more influenced by the appearance of food than others. In one study, she showed that the sight and smell of a sizzling steak can directly raise the insulin levels in the blood of people who had earlier been identified as "externals"; in other words, they responded more to external or environmental food cues than did most people. **(Psychology of motivation)**

8. Two eating disorders that are prevalent in today's society are anorexia nervosa and bulimia nervosa. Anorexia is a disorder in which people fear becoming obese and radically decrease their food intake, even to the point of emaciation. Bulimia is a disorder in which a person eats excessively, and soon thereafter vomits or uses laxatives to eliminate the food from the body. Such problems are much more prevalent among females than males. **(Eating disorders)**

9. By means of directly observing volunteers in a university laboratory, Masters and Johnson identified the following four stages of the sexual response cycle: arousal, plateau, orgasm, and resolution. The only identified difference between men and women is that women are capable of multiple orgasms, whereas men have a refractory period in the resolution period during which they cannot ejaculate again until the body is physiologically prepared. **(Sexual motivation)**

10. External stimuli are especially important in sexual motivation in humans, whereas in most mammals, such as dogs, hormones play a bigger influence in the determination of when they have intercourse. External stimuli, such as particular types of clothing, hair color, or body build can play a strong role in the determination of what people find to be arousing. By means of classical conditioning, operant conditioning, or modeling, a person learns to respond to certain external stimuli. **(Sexual motivation)**

11. Achievement motivation describes a person's needs to reach goals and master skills. People can have low, medium, or high needs for achievement. Need for achievement is sometimes studied by having people give a storyline to an ambiguous picture. Intrinsic motivation is the internal desire to accomplish something for the sake of accomplishing it, whether or not the goal results in food, money, or some other pleasurable reward. In contrast, extrinsic motivation is the desire to accomplish something to gain a tangible reward or to avoid being punished. **(Achievement motivation)**

12. Physiological arousal takes place when a person is emotionally aroused. The autonomic nervous system controls arousal and allows the body to prepare for action. For example, the liver releases sugar into the bloodstream when extra energy is needed. Fear and rage produce different physiological changes compared to happiness and joy. **(Physiology of emotion)**

13. People sometimes use the same gestures in different cultures to mean very different things. However, people in different cultures tend to experience facial emotions, such as smiling or frowning, in surprisingly similar ways. Even though people seem to speak a universal language with facial muscles, cultures differ widely in the extent to which it is acceptable to show certain emotions, or to be emotionally expressive at all. **(Expressing emotion)**

14. People communicate in verbal ways, using words, and in nonverbal ways, too. Nonverbal ways include body stance and posture, for example. By varying the extent of a facial look, a person can communicate a variety of emotions from intimacy to dominance to anger and frustration. Psychologists have discovered that specific facial muscles, such as those that control movement of the eyebrows, are related to specific types of emotions. **(Expressing emotion)**

15. According to the James-Lange theory of emotion, the body responds physiologically, and that causes the person to have the emotion. In contrast, according to the Cannon-Bard theory, physiological responses sometimes occur too slowly to allow one to note what emotion he or she is experiencing. Instead, the physiological response and the emotion occur together, but one does not cause the other. **(Theories of emotion)**

16. Most psychologists today adhere to Schachter's Two-Factor theory of emotion. According to the two-factor theory, there are two parts of emotion. First of all, an emotion starts to grow from the sense that one is physiologically aroused. Next, one has a cognitive awareness and calls the emotion by some

label. Thus, Schachter's theory is a combination of the James-Lange and the Cannon-Bard theory. When a person is physiologically aroused due to exercise, but a potential sexual partner is on the stationary bicycle next to them at the gym, they might actually label the arousal as attraction. **(Theories of emotion)**

17. The role of thought, or cognition, appears to play an important part in emotion. That implies that a person can change an emotion by changing his or her thoughts. **(Cognition and emotion)**

18. People are biologically prepared to learn to fear some things more than others, probably for the sake of survival. The amygdala in the brain plays a role in learning fear responses. Research has shown a genetic component to fear. Identical twins—even those raised in different homes—have similar levels of fearfulness. **(Physiology of emotion)**

19. Happiness is an area that has been studied less than the negative emotions. Research has shown that happiness comes and goes, and that most people are happy only some of the time. People who have sudden good fortune, such as after winning a lottery, find that after the initial thrill disappears, the overall level of happiness in their lives seems to be about the same as before winning. All around the world it has been found that wealthy people are not much happier than the people who just barely have enough to buy necessities. According the the Facial Feedback Hypothesis, if a person smiles, it is more likely to lead to a sense of feeling happy, even if the person is not initially feeling very "upbeat," due to the effect that feedback from the muscles has on the brain. **(Experienced emotions)**

20. Anger is less likely to be expressed in places such as Tahiti and Japan. It has been found that when people vent anger, it can make them calm temporarily, but it can also lead to feelings of guilt and anxiety, or even increased levels of anger. Psychologists say that it is probably better to wait before expressing anger, giving the body a chance to calm down physiologically. It has also been suggested to release anger by means of exercising, writing in a diary, or letting it out in the company of a trusted friend. **(Experienced emotions)**

21. According to the Adaptation-Level Principle, people are likely to evaluate stimuli relative to previous life experiences. In other words, people get used to things, and develop tolerance, such as to having electric lights or a color television set, and then something even more exciting must occur before it seems other than normal. Whether we feel satisfied or not is relative to our past experiences. Similarly, the Relative Deprivation Principle states that another component of happiness has to do with those around us that we compare ourselves to, and whether or not we think they are worse off than we are. If a person makes comparisons with less well-off people, he or she will feel happier, but if a person makes comparisons with those who are wealthier or more successful, he or she will likely feel envious. **(Theories of emotion)**

Grade Yourself

Circle the numbers of the questions you missed, then fill in the total incorrect for each topic. If you answered more than three questions incorrectly, you need to focus on that topic. (If a topic has less than three questions and you had at least one wrong, we suggest you study that topic also. Read your textbook, a review book, or ask your teacher for help.)

Subject: Motivation and Emotion

Topic	Question Numbers	Number Incorrect
Heirarchy of motives	1	
Physiology of motivation	2, 4, 5, 6	
Theories of motivation	3	
Psychology of motivation	7	
Eating disorders	8	
Sexual motivation	9, 10	
Achievement motivation	11	
Physiology of emotion	12, 18	
Expressing emotion	13, 14	
Theories of emotion	15, 16, 21	
Cognition and emotion	17	
Experienced emotion	19, 20	

Personality

14

Brief Yourself

An individual's personality is composed of patterns of feeling, behaving, and thinking. The study of personality emphasizes the individual person. There are four main views of personality, including the psychoanalytic theory, the trait view, the humanistic approach, and the social-cognitive approach. Personality changes across the lifespan, and can be influenced by learning, motivation, and society. A person's personality can also affect his or her health. Some people have personality disorders to the extent that they cause problems in living.

Test Yourself

1. Give a brief biographical sketch of Sigmund Freud.

2. What does psychoanalysis involve?

3. Describe Freud's view of the human personality. In his opinion, what does personality consist of?

4. What is the unconscious mind, and how does it differ from the subconscious?

5. Describe the five psychosexual stages of development.

6. What are defense mechanisms, in general, and what are some of the specific defense mechanisms Freud described?

7. Who is responsible for the idea of the collective unconscious, and what did he mean by it?

8. What are projective personality tests? Give some examples.

9. Describe trait theory.

10. What is the Eysenck Personality Questionnaire?

11. What is a personality inventory? Give examples and tell how they are used.

12. Describe the humanistic perspective of personality.

13. What is self-actualization? Who proposed this idea in the field of personality?

14. Who developed the person-centered perspective, and what is it?

15. Describe the social-cognitive perspective of personality.

16. Summarize the research on personal control.

17. Compare and contrast learned helplessness with personal control.

18. How did psychologists Adler and Horney feel about Freud's ideas concerning personality?

19. Critique the Rorschach test.

20. Provide some basic criticisms of Freud's personality theory.

Check Yourself

1. Sigmund Freud attended the University of Vienna in the late 1800s. After graduating from medical school, he started a private practice, specializing in the treatment of nervous disorders. Soon he began to encounter patients with no apparent, underlying, physical cause for their disorder, and he began to investigate the possibility of psychological, as well as physical, causes for nervous disorders. He used hypnosis and dream analysis, and developed free association as a way of looking at the unconscious, and ultimately, as a way to expose underlying psychological problems. **(Freud)**

2. Psychoanalysis involves an exploration of the unconscious by a trained psychotherapist. The technique was originated by Sigmund Freud, and includes the use of hypnotism, dream analysis, and free association. Using free association, the patient is asked to say whatever comes to mind, no matter what the topic. Freud thought that free association would free up a chain of thoughts, including painful memories and childhood experiences, leading to the person's unconscious mind. **(Psychoanalysis)**

3. According to Freud, personality consists of the id, ego, and superego. These are constructs that are not parts of the brain, per se. The id is present at birth, and operates according to the Pleasure Principle, by means of which the child tries to get needs satisfied in a self-centered way. As the child gets older, the ego appears. The ego is the rational part of the personality and operates according to the Reality Principle. On the other end of the spectrum is the superego, which serves as the conscience, telling the person what is right and what is wrong, in an ethical sense. The superego is the last component of the personality to develop. The ego struggles between the id and superego, to decide what is best for the person, and to help the person function in a society. Freud believed that the bulk of personality is "beneath the surface," hidden from a person's conscious awareness. **(Personality components)**

4. The unconscious mind, in Freud's theory, is the collection of thoughts and desires that are typically unacceptable to the person, but the person does not realize such thoughts and desires are present, as he or she is unaware of them. Although the person is not aware of unconscious thoughts, such thoughts can influence behavior without the person's knowledge. The preconscious part of the mind is that which contains material that can be willfully brought up into conscious awareness. **(Personality components)**

5. The five psychosexual stages of development include: the oral stage, which lasts from birth until about eighteen months of age; the anal stage, which lasts from eighteen months to three years of age; the phallic stage, from three to six years of age; the latency stage, from about six to pubery; and the genital stage, which starts at the time of puberty and continues thereafter. According to Freud's view, humans derive pleasure from a specific area of the body for each stage of development. During the oral stage, the baby's focus is on obtaining pleasure from the mouth. Similarly, during the anal stage the child obtains gratification from bodily functions that involve bladder and bowel activities. During the phallic stage, young boys experience the Oedipus complex, while young girls experience the Electra complex. Both involve sexual attraction for the parent of the opposite sex, and resentment of the same-sex parent. During latency, sexual desires become repressed; and during the genital stage, sexual interests arise again, but

become mature and adultlike in nature. Fixations can occur at any of the stages. (**Personality development**)

6. A defense mechanism is the method the ego uses to protect itself unconsciously from anxiety. Defense mechanisms involve a distortion of reality. Some of the more-common defense mechanisms include: repression, in which thoughts are kept from entering conscious awareness; rationalization, in which a person comes up with reasons for his or her own behavior that sound logical, but that are incorrect, or only partially correct; and displacement, in which an aggressive or sexual feeling is moved from the unacceptable object that brought about the desire to an object that is considered to be "safe" or socially acceptable. For example, if one is angry at the boss, one is more likely to blame and yell at one's spouse, rather than directly address the boss. Regression is a defense mechanism in which a person acts in an immature way that would have been appropriate as a child, for example. (**Defense mechanisms**)

7. Jung is responsible for the idea of the collective unconscious. It is the idea that all human beings share an unconscious that is inherited and goes back to common experiences that our early ancestors had. (**Jung**)

8. Projective personality tests involve the technique of showing the person ambiguous information, such as a picture. The client is asked to say what that picture looks like to him or her, or the client might be asked to make up a story about it. The therapist can learn about the client from the response he or she "projects" on to the picture. Examples of projective tests are the Thematic Apperception Test (TAT) and Rorschach ink blot test. (**Projective tests**)

9. Trait theory, developed by Allport, describes personality in terms of key traits, or characteristic behavior patterns that are conscious, rather than unconscious. The ancient Greeks described personality by means of types, such as sanguine, melancholic, phlegmatic, and choleric, in a related way. (**Trait theory**)

10. The Eysenck Personality Questionnaire is based on the idea that many of a person's individual variations can be reduced to two primary dimensions or factors, by means of which most types of personality traits can be described. The two key personality factors, according to Hans and Sybil Eysenck, are stability/instability and extroversion/introversion. Other psychologists prefer to describe personality in terms of five factors, including emotional stability, extroversion, openness, agreeableness, and conscientiousness, termed the "Big Five" Personality Factors. (**Personality factors**)

11. Personality inventories are often long questionnaires that are used to assess several personality traits at once. One of the most widely used inventories to assess psychological disorders is the Minnesota Multiphasic Personality Inventory (MMPI). The MMPI-2, in use today, contains ten clinical scales, along with validity scales. In addition, it contains fifteen content scales to assess family problems, etc. Personality inventories are scored objectively, providing numerical scores on each scale, avoiding the need for subjective impressions on the part of the therapist. (**MMPI**)

12. The humanistic perspective developed partially in response to dissatisfaction with both Freud's sexual and sexist view of personality and the somewhat sterile, trait perspective. Humanist personality psychologists advocated the view of people as "whole" beings, who are more than a sum of test scores and as "healthy" beings, who are more than frustrated, repressed neurotics. The humanistic perspective emphasizes human potential for growth through the eyes of the person, rather than from the viewpoint of the therapist. (**Humanistic view**)

13. Maslow developed his ideas of personality through the study of psychologically healthy people. Maslow thought that people experience a hierarchy of needs, from the basic needs for food and shelter, to the more complex need for self-actualization. Self-actualization involves the development of mature qualities, such as being self-accepting, open, loving, and living up to one's potential. (**Self-actualization**)

14. The person-centered perspective was developed by Carl Rogers. Rogers, a humanistic psychologist, believed that humans are basically good and will move toward growth and self-actualization whenever possible. Rogers promoted a therapeutic environment, in which the therapist exhibits qualities of genuineness, empathy, and acceptance, including what he called unconditional positive regard for the client. **(Person-centered perspective)**

15. The social-cognitive perspective is composed of elements of cognition, learning, and social psychology. Bandura said that many behaviors are learned by means of classical and operant conditioning, and also through modeling. Interwoven with learning are the influences of a person's thoughts and reactions to the environment. In a way, we create our environment, yet we are also created by it, which Bandura referred to as "reciprocal determinism." **(Social-cognitive perspective)**

16. A sense of personal control is part of a person's personality. Personal control involves the degree to which a person feels as if he or she can do something about the world and the situations one ends up in. Behavior is influenced by the sense of an external versus internal locus of self-control. An external locus of control means that the person feels as though outside forces, such as luck or fate, determine what will happen to him or her, whereas an internal locus means that the person feels as though he or she controls his or her own fate. **(Personal control)**

17. Learned helplessness is a feeling of a lack of personal control. Learned helplessness results when a person or animal attempts to influence the environment, such as to get out of a physically or emotionally painful situation, only to discover that he or she cannot do it. Over time and after several trials, this tends to result in despair and passively giving up. When new hope is presented, no attempt is made to influence the situation, or "escape." **(Personal control)**

18. Adler and Horney are called "neo-Freudians," in that they agreed with Freud in some ways. For example, they both felt that childhood is important to personality development. Unlike Freud, however, they believed social tensions and struggles during childhood were more important than sexual ones. They also emphasized the importance of the conscious mind more than Freud did. **(Personality development)**

19, Researchers think that the Rorschach projective test lacks reliability and validity. It lacks a single scoring method. Although it is not as popular as it used to be, some psychologists still find it to be helpful. **(Projective tests)**

20. Freudian theory is not completely scientific. Instead, his theory is subjective, more than objective, proposes very few testable hypotheses, and gives after-the-fact explanations of behavior, rather than making predictions. **(Freud)**

Grade Yourself

Circle the numbers of the questions you missed, then fill in the total incorrect for each topic. If you answered more than three questions incorrectly, you need to focus on that topic. (If a topic has less than three questions and you had at least one wrong, we suggest you study that topic also. Read your textbook, a review book, or ask your teacher for help.)

Subject: Personality

Topic	Question Numbers	Number Incorrect
Freud	1, 20	
Psychoanalysis	2	
Personality components	3, 4	
Personality development	5, 18	
Defense mechanisms	6	
Jung	7	
Projective tests	8, 19	
Trait theory	9	
Personality factors	10	
MMPI	11	
Humanistic view	12	
Self-actualization	13	
Person-centered perspective	14	
Social-cognitive perspective	15	
Personal control	16, 17	

Psychological Disorders

15

Brief Yourself

Numerous psychological problems have been identified by psychologists. No matter what the disorder, it can be looked at from different perspectives, in an attempt to explain and treat it. The perspective based on the assumption that psychological disorders are illnesses is that of the medical model. The medical model emphasizes a biological look at the disorder. Psychiatrists are more likely to take the medical approach. In contrast, psychologists who adhere to social-cultural perspectives tend to believe that psychological problems are often problems related to society and one's culture. In this chapter, a number of psychological problems will be examined.

Test Yourself

1. What is the DSM-IV? Mention why it was developed.

2. Describe major depression and mention something about the incidence of occurrence.

3. Compare the biological explanation of mood disorder with the social-cognitive perspective.

4. How is bipolar disorder different from major depression?

5. Compare and contrast the somatoform disorders of conversion and hypochondriasis. Which of the two was prevalent in Freud's day, but is now rare?

6. Discuss anxiety disorders and mention specific types.

7. Describe the phobic disorder and give some examples of phobias.

8. What are some common explanations for how phobias come about?

9. How are phobic disorders different from generalized anxiety disorder?

10. Describe the obsessive-compulsive disorder. Include the difference between an obsession and a compulsion.

11. Explain what a dissociative disorder is and give three examples of types of dissociative disorders.

12. What is psychogenic amnesia? How is psychogenic amnesia different from amnesia that results from a blow to the head or a blackout after binging on alcohol?

13. Compare and contrast fugue with psychogenic amnesia.

14. Describe the multiple personality.

15. Give some examples of well-known cases of multiple personality. What appears to be partially responsible for its development?

16. What is the category of psychological problem referred to as a personality disorder? How is a personality disorder different from most other psychological problems?

17. Give two examples of a personality disorder and compare them.

18. What is considered to be the most serious psychological problem of them all? Why?

19. Mention and explain three of the key symptoms of schizophrenia.

20. What is the difference between a positive and negative symptom of schizophrenia?

21. How are brain abnormalities thought to play a role in schizophrenia?

22. Explain how genetics plays a role in schizophrenia.

23. What psychological factors are considered high-risk in regard to the development of schizophrenia? Provide an explanation of psychological factors that can play a role in its appearance.

Check Yourself

1. The DSM-IV is the Diagnostic and Statistical Manual of Mental Disorders (fourth edition)—a book that classifies and describes symptoms of psychological disorders. The DSM-IV was developed by psychologists and psychiatrists, in conjunction with the World Health Organization. The DSM-IV uses a multi-axial system, to group about 230 different disorders into a logical order. Most insurance companies in the United States require a diagnosis from this book before covering therapeutic sessions. **(DSM-IV)**

2. Major depression is a mood disorder in which a person feels despondent and hopeless. Most people get depressed, such as a result of a loss or a bad grade, and pull out of it within a day to a month. In contrast, people with major depression stay depressed and can't seem to pull out of it. People with major depression often cannot identify any specific problem that might have brought about the discouragement and lethargy. Major depression is about twice as likely to occur in females, as compared to males, and it is so prevalent in the United States that it is sometimes referred to as the "common cold" of psychological problems. **(Mood disorders)**

3. The biological explanation of mood disorder examines genetic influences and biochemical factors. Genetically, mood disorders have been found to run in families. Biochemically, it has been found that neurotransmitters in the brain play a role. People who are depressed tend to have a lack of norepinephrine and a lack of serotonin. According to the social-cognitive perspective, thoughts and beliefs can also play a role in depression. **(Mood disorders)**

4. Major depression involves becoming depressed and staying in that state until, or if, one comes out of it. In contrast, bipolar disorder, or manic depression, involves a period of major depression, but the person then enters a manic state, in which he or she is hyperactive, overly optimistic, talks excessively, and is elated. In the bipolar disorder, with fluctuations between depression and mania, the person finds it hard to carry on in day-to-day life, as he or she is unpredictable to others. Lithium is the preferred treatment to help the person with bipolar disorder remain in a steady state. **(Mood disorders)**

5. The somatoform disorder is a psychological problem that manifests itself in the person's body, as physical problems that have no real biological explanation. One type is the conversion disorder, which was much more common in Freud's day. In the conversion disorder, a person is anxious about something, and that psychological anxiety is changed, or converted, into a physical problem with no known physical cause. For example, anxiety about giving a piano recital might make a person's hands appear to be paralyzed, to the point that even poking the person's hand with pins does not cause him or her to flinch. In contrast, hypochondriasis is a fairly common problem, in which a person has a physical symptom, such as a headache, but seeks out doctor after doctor, to confirm that it is symptomatic of a brain tumor, or some other dread disease. Hypochondriacs are often seeking attention by blowing a small physical problem out of proportion. **(Somatoform disorders)**

6. Anxiety disorders are those that involve heightened nervous system arousal. Various types include generalized anxiety disorder, phobias, and the obsessive-compulsive disorder. **(Anxiety disorders)**

7. A phobic disorder is a type of anxiety disorder in which the anxiety is involved in fear of a specific object or situation. The person knows exactly what he or she fears, but the fear becomes irrational, to the point that the person might walk a mile out of the way just to avoid a dog behind a fence. Examples of some of the more-common phobias include the fears of height, flying, closed spaces, animals, insects, and thunder/lightning. **(Anxiety disorders)**

8. Psychologists think that phobias are learned behaviors and can be unlearned by means of counter-conditioning and systematic descensitization. (**Anxiety disorders**)

9. Phobias bring about anxiety related to a very specific object or event, whereas the generalized anxiety disorder involves anxiety that the person cannot find a reason for. People with generalized anxiety disorder tend to have clammy palms, be nervous and edgy much of the time, experience dizziness and a racing heart. This is referred to as free-floating anxiety, because no particular stimulus brings it about. These people also are likely candidates for a panic attack— a brief period in which they experience strong fear for no apparent reason. (**Anxiety disorders**)

10. Obsessive-compulsive disorders also fall into the category of anxiety disorder. An obsession is a thought that comes back repeatedly, and a compulsion is an action that the person does again and again. A person with an obsessive-compulsive disorder is unable to stop the thoughts and repetitive actions. It seems that the repetition helps relieve the anxiety. Common obsessions include thoughts about dirt, thoughts about death, and concern over exactness. Common compulsions include checking doors, locks, and appliances, and excessive handwashing. (**Anxiety disorders**)

11. Dissociative disorders are rare. They are called "dissociative" because under stress, conscious awareness becomes separated from painful memories and thoughts. Three types of dissociative disorders include psychogenic amnesia, fugue, and multiple personality. (**Dissociative disorders**)

12. Psychogenic amnesia is different from the amnesia that results when a person experiences a blow to the head, because it has a psychological, rather than a physical, cause. In psychogenic amnesia, the person cannot remember certain things, and the memory loss is selective. For example, the person would be likely to forget key aspects of an auto accident in which someone was killed, but still remember how to add and who is president. (**Dissociative disorders**)

13. Whereas psychogenic amnesia is the inability to recall traumatic events, fugue involves forgetting, plus leaving one's home and job, and abruptly starting a new life, without recollection of the old one. (**Dissociative disorders**)

14. Multiple personality is a very controversial psychological problem. People with multiple personalities have several unique personalities all contained within the same body. These people are seldom violent. Sometimes the person is aware of some of the other personalities, but other times not. (**Dissociative disorders**)

15. The books, *The Three Faces of Eve*, and *Sybil* present two case studies of women with multiple personalities. Psychologists have found that for people with multiple personalities, it is common to have been severely abused, or even tortured, as a child. (**Dissociative disorders**)

16. A personality disorder is a type of problem with patterns of behavior that impair a person's social contacts. They sometimes co-occur with other psychological problems, but they are unique in that they are very difficult to change and start early in childhood. (**Personality disorders**)

17. Two examples of personality disorders include the histrionic personality disorder, in which the person seeks the praise and attention of others, but is shallow, and doesn't give much back to others when it comes to emotional support. The histrionic wants to be the "star of the show," and is often promiscuous. Another type of personality disorder is the antisocial personality, sometimes referred to as the psychopath or sociopath. The antisocial personality is almost always a man, whereas the histrionic personality is almost always a woman. The person with the antisocial personality disorder has no conscience, will cheat

anyone, including family members, and often becomes a con artist, moving from town to town, never feeling sorry for hurting others. **(Personality disorders)**

18. Schizophrenia is considered to be the most-serious psychological problem of all. At the present time, medications can keep it under control to some degree, but there is no cure. The symptoms of schizophrenia greatly disrupt the person's life, often appearing in adolescence or early adulthood. In schizophrenia, there is a split from reality, which is considered to be psychotic. However, schizophrenia does not mean that the person has more than one personality. **(Schizophrenia)**

19. Three key categories of symptoms of schizophrenia include: inappropriate emotions/actions, disorganized thought patterns, and disrupted perceptions. Inappropriate emotions are seen when the schizophrenic laughs at things others find sad, and vice versa. Inappropriate actions are seen in rocking back and forth uncontrollably, for example, or holding a pose in a catatonic manner for long periods of time. Disorganized thought can be seen in the lack of ability to carry on a logical conversation and the tendency to have false beliefs (delusions), such as the belief that one is a famous person. Finally, disturbed perceptions include hallucinations that are typically auditory in nature. **(Schizophrenia)**

20. Positive symptoms in schizophrenia include things the person does, such as laughing inappropriately, talking in ways that don't make sense, or rubbing one's skin until it becomes raw. In contrast, negative symptoms are those that show a lack of responding, such as a face without emotion, or a rigid body, or a voice with no expression. **(Schizophrenia)**

21. Brain abnormalities have been found to play a role in schizophrenia. Schizophrenics tend to have an excess amount of the neurotransmitter dopamine. They also often have abnormal brain tissue, a comparative lack of brain activity in the frontal lobes, plus shrinkage of cortical tissue. **(Schizophrenia)**

22. Genetics also plays a role in schizophrenia, as it runs in families, and the chances of becoming schizophrenic are much higher if one has an identical twin or a parent with the disorder. **(Schizophrenia)**

23. Psychological factors play a role in schizophrenia, too. Even if a person has a genetic predisposition for the disorder, it often takes a psychological problem, such as high stress, to trigger it. It has also been found that birth complications, low birth weight, separation from parents during childhood, short attention span, and disruptive behavior during childhood are somehow related to the later development of schizophrenia, but at this point the exact roles the psychological factors play are unknown. **(Schizophrenia)**

Grade Yourself

Circle the numbers of the questions you missed, then fill in the total incorrect for each topic. If you answered more than three questions incorrectly, you need to focus on that topic. (If a topic has less than three questions and you had at least one wrong, we suggest you study that topic also. Read your textbook, a review book, or ask your teacher for help.)

Subject: Psychological Disorders

Topic	Question Numbers	Number Incorrect
DSM-IV	1	
Mood disorders	2, 3, 4	
Somatoform disorders	5	
Anxiety disorders	6, 7, 8, 9, 10	
Dissociative disorders	11, 12, 13, 14, 15	
Personality disorders	16, 17	
Schizophrenia	18, 19, 20, 21, 22, 23	

Psychotherapy

16

Brief Yourself

At this point in history, psychologists are getting a better idea of how to treat psychological problems. In earlier centuries, those with psychological disorders were often punished and treated harshly, often as a result of the belief that they were possessed by demons. As an outgrowth of reforms made by Dorothea Dix and by Philippe Pinel, mental hospitals were built to treat those with disorders in a more humane way. With the advent of medications to treat psychological disorders in the 1950s, fewer people were put into mental hospitals. Today there are many forms of treatment available. Psychiatrists and psychologists use a variety of techniques, including medication, and/or psychological approaches that involve a verbal interaction between the therapist and client. Such psychological approaches include psychoanalysis, humanistic therapies, behavior therapies, cognitive therapies, and group therapies.

Test Yourself

1. Describe the psychoanalytic therapeutic technique.

2. What are some common criticisms of psychoanalysis?

3. What do biomedical therapies involve?

4. Mention some of the pros and cons of using antipsychotic drugs to treat people.

5. How do some of the more common antidepressant drugs work?

6. How does electroconvulsive therapy work?

7. Describe psychosurgery, and include a discussion of lobotomy.

8. What is the basic approach of behavior therapy?

9. Describe the use of classical conditioning for therapeutic purposes.

10. How can operant conditioning be used as therapy?

11. What is a token economy? Where is a token economy likely to be used?

12. As a therapist, how would you use the technique of systematic desensitization? Pick a psychological problem and tell how you would proceed to treat it with this method.

13. How is systematic desensitization different from aversive therapy?

14. What is humanistic therapy?

15. Describe Carl Rogers's form of humanistic therapy, and provide its name.

16. Describe the Gestalt approach of Fritz Perls.

17. What is cognitive therapy?

18. How does cognitive therapy differ from behavior approaches?

19. What is rational-emotive therapy? Who created this approach?

20. Give a brief description of group therapy, and mention different types.

Check Yourself

1. Psychoanalysis is based on the work of Freud. A key assumption is that psychological problems are a result of repressed conflicts that stay in the unconscious beginning in childhood. The patient is encouraged to free-associate, or say whatever comes to mind. Dream analysis is another way to examine the unconscious. In traditional psychoanalysis, which continues over a number of years, it is the patient who does most of the talking. **(Psychoanalysis)**

2. Some have criticized psychoanalysis, due to its time-consuming and expensive nature. Some also criticize the strong emphasis placed on childhood and early experiences. Some also mention the lack of scientific evidence, as it is impossible to test the Freudian principles psychoanalysis is based on. **(Psychoanalysis)**

3. Biomedical therapies are based on the idea that psychological problems have a biological cause, as with any illness. Biomedical therapies include the use of a variety of antipsychotic drugs, the use of electroconvulsive therapy, and the use of psychosurgery. **(Biomedical therapy)**

4. Antipsychotic drugs were discovered in the 1950s. The introduction allowed many people to leave mental hospitals and live more normal lives. Drug therapy also reduced the number of people subjected to psychosurgery. Specifically, antipsychotic drugs, such as thorazine and cloazapine, have been used to treat the very serious problem of schizophrenia. Long-term use of antipsychotic drugs can lead to twitching of facial muscles, dry mouth, sleep disturbances, and tremors. **(Drug therapy)**

5. Some common antidepressants in use today are Prozac, Zoloft, and Paxil. They work by inhibiting the re-uptake of serotonin by neurotransmitters in the brain. It takes about two to four weeks for an antidepressant's effects to be felt by the patient. Bipolar disorders are treated with lithium. **(Drug therapy)**

6. Electroconvulsive therapy, or ECT, is very controversial in its manipulation of the brain, and is considered by some to be barbaric. Introduced in the 1930s, it is typically used to treat severely depressed people. The patient is given a general anesthetic and a muscle relaxant, followed by a very brief and strong electric shock to the brain. A series of about six to twelve treatments is commonly given over the course of two to four weeks. How ECT works is not precisely known. One of the many side effects includes memory disturbance. **(Electroconvulsive therapy)**

7. Psychosurgery is used either to remove or to destroy brain tissue. Probably the most famous technique, the lobotomy, was developed in the 1930s. The surgeon, Moniz, developed the technique in which the nerves that connected the frontal lobes and the parts of the brain that control emotion, were severed. The technique was typically used on violent people and those with uncontrollable emotions. The result was a person who permanently became immature and lethargic. Today, lobotomies are rarely performed. Other forms of psychosurgery are also rarely used. **(Psychosurgery)**

8. Behavior therapy utilizes the fundamentals of learning theory to help people change unwanted behaviors. Behavior therapy uses classical and operant conditioning, and has the most success with problems such as anxiety, fear, and some sexual dysfunctions. **(Behavior therapy)**

9. Classical conditioning techniques for the alteration of behavior are based on the principles discovered by Ivan Pavlov. As Pavlov and others have pointed out, both desirable and undesirable behaviors are learned. If a person's fear of water can be seen as a conditioned response that comes about as a result of the stimuli of smelling the ocean or seeing sand or hearing the sound of a JetSki, then a person can learn to respond to the smell of the ocean with a new response pattern, as opposed to fear. Counterconditioning is a technique in which the person pairs a new response, such as relaxation, with the originally

anxiety-provoking stimulus. A popular form of counterconditioning is systematic desensitization. Extinction can be used, as well as aversive techniques. (**Classical conditioning therapies**)

10. Operant conditioning, based on discoveries by B. F. Skinner and others, can also be used to change behaviors through re-learning, but in this case the behaviors are voluntary, as opposed to the reflexive ones involved in classical conditioning. Using principles of operant conditioning, the therapist reinforces desired behaviors and punishes, or at least withholds reinforcement, for undesired ones. (**Operant conditioning therapies**)

11. A token economy is the technique of using rewards to modify a person's behavior. Token economies are often used in psychiatric hospitals or in institutions for developmentally disabled people. A token economy can also be used by parents in the home, or by a teacher at a school. Using a token economy, when the patient displays a desired behavior, such as making her or his bed, the therapist or therapist's assistant provides the person with a poker chip, for example, that can be saved up and exchanged later for television-viewing privileges, snacks, etc. (**Operant conditioning therapies**)

12. Systematic desensitization is commonly used to treat phobias, or irrational fears. The technique involves first training the client to relax, by means of progressive relaxation. The client relaxes muscle groups throughout the body, say, starting with the shoulders and moving on down to the feet. The therapist talks the person through the relaxation, until he or she is able to proceed on his or her own. In another session, the therapist would introduce a topic that is fearful to the client, having first established a hierarchy of fears for that individual. For example, if the client is afraid of elevators, the therapist might simply mention an elevator, and the client would practice relaxation. Each time, the therapist mentions more and more fearful situations, and eventually takes the person to look at an actual elevator, and then for a ride in the elevator. The process could take a period of several weeks or months. Systematic desensitization has been very successful in the treatment of phobias. (**Systematic desensitization**)

13. Systematic desensitization differs from aversive therapy, in that aversive therapy is the opposite of systematic desensitization. Using aversive therapy, the psychologist attempts to replace a positive response or feeling that is associated with a harmful stimulus, with that of a negative response or feeling. For example, an aversion therapy program might involve having an alcoholic take a daily medication (Antabuse) that causes nausea in a person upon drinking alcohol. Whereas the alcoholic would originally have learned positive associations with alcohol, the alcoholic would come to have negative associations with it. (**Aversion therapy**)

14. Humanistic therapy uses techniques that place an emphasis on the client's potential for self-fulfillment and growth. The therapist believes in this inner potential and emphasizes the person's self-worth, helping a person to grow in self-awareness and acceptance. Humanistic therapy concentrates on the present as opposed to the past, on conscious awareness, and on taking responsibility for one's situation. (**Humanistic therapy**)

15. Carl Rogers's form of humanistic therapy is called Person-Centered Therapy. It places an emphasis on the way that a person thinks about himself or herself. The therapist avoids making value judgments. This approach is nondirective in nature. According to Rogers, three characteristics of an effective therapist include genuineness, accurate empathy, and unconditional positive regard. (**Person-centered therapy**)

16. Gestalt therapy is a type of humanistic therapy developed by Fritz Perls that encourages the client to get in touch with himself or herself, to take responsibility in the here and now, and to express one's feelings. Gestalt therapists also believe in the power of actions to influence one's thoughts and feelings. A Gestalt therapist might ask a client to participate in role-play as an exercise. (**Gestalt therapy**)

17. Cognitive therapy is based on the assumption that a person's thought patterns influence his or her feelings. **(Cognitive therapy)**

18. Cognitive therapy has been more successful with problems such as depression or generalized anxiety, whereas behavior therapy has had a higher success rate with specific phobias. **(Cognitive therapy)**

19. Rational emotive therapy, or RET, was created by Albert Ellis. RET assumes that numerous psychological problems come about as a result of irrational thoughts. Using this approach, the therapist would challenge a person's irrational ideas, such as the idea that he or she is unlovable, because a partner broke up with him or her, or that he or she will never find satisfactory work, because of being fired from a current job. **(Rational emotive therapy)**

20. Group therapy is cost-effective. The sessions cost less, and the therapist is able to see more people at one time. Instead of one therapist working together with one client, a single therapist meets with a group of clients who all have a similar problem. A group situation can help a person realize that he or she is not alone. Encounter groups encourage open talk about emotionally charged experiences. Support groups, such as those for divorced people, alcoholics, or widowers can help, too. A type of group therapy called family therapy involves a therapist's interactions with the entire family, to examine how everyone might play a role in a problem, such as the teen's truancy, or the mother's bad temper, or the father's tendency to stay away from home. **(Group therapy)**

Grade Yourself

Circle the numbers of the questions you missed, then fill in the total incorrect for each topic. If you answered more than three questions incorrectly, you need to focus on that topic. (If a topic has less than three questions and you had at least one wrong, we suggest you study that topic also. Read your textbook, a review book, or ask your teacher for help.)

Subject: Psychotherapy

Topic	Question Numbers	Number Incorrect
Psychoanalysis	1, 2	
Biomedical therapy	3	
Drug therapy	4, 5	
Electroconvulsive therapy	6	
Psychosurgery	7	
Behavior therapy	8	
Classical conditioning therapies	9	
Operant conditioning therapies	10, 11	
Systematic desensitization	12	
Aversion therapy	13	
Humanistic therapy	14	
Person-centered therapy	15	
Gestalt therapy	16	
Cognitive therapy	17, 18	
Rational emotive therapy	19	
Group therapy	20	

Stress and Health

Brief Yourself

A person's lifestyle can affect his or her health. A lifestyle that involves severe stress over a long period can cause impairment in both psychological and physical well-being. When stimulated by stressors, the autonomic nervous system creates changes in the normal activities of numerous organs. Stress can be a result of both positive and negative events. It can also be a result of choices, such as diet, physical fitness, alcohol or drug abuse, and taking sexual risks. The area of health psychology looks at the influence of lifestyle, emotions, personality, and situations on the amount of stress experienced.

Test Yourself

1. What is stress?

2. What is the stress response system?

3. What body activities typically change as a result of stress?

4. Describe Selye's work on stress.

5. Describe the General Adaptation Syndrome in detail.

6. Give some examples of both positive and negative stressful life events.

7. What are the differences between the biological and psychological affects of stress?

8. How does one's sense of control play a role in the experience of stress?

9. Describe personality "types" and their influence on health.

10. Give a brief description of the functioning of the immune system.

11. How can aerobic exercise help combat stress?

12. Describe ways to practice relaxation.

13. How can social support be effective in the reduction of stress?

14. How does biofeedback play a role in stress reduction?

15. How does cigarette smoking affect the body? Give details.

16. Discuss the effectiveness of programs to help people stop smoking.

17. How does nutrition play a role in combating stress?

18. Discuss obesity and its relationship to health.

19. If a person decides to reduce his or her weight, what is the best way to proceed?

20. How do genetics and culture interrelate to play a role in determining body weight?

Check Yourself

1. Stress consists of a pattern of responses. These responses are physiological, behavioral, cognitive, and emotional, and they result due to either real stimuli or imagined ones. The stimuli are perceived to threaten a person's well-being. Sometimes they are perceived as preventing a person from accomplishing a goal. **(Definition of stress)**

2. The stress response system is the body's physical response to stress that is governed by the autonomic nervous system. The autonomic nervous system is controlled by the hypothalamus gland. When a person feels the emotion of the stress, the hypothalamus sends out signals to the autonomic nervous system and to the pituitary gland. As a result, body organs are "told" to change normal activities. **(Definition of stress)**

3. As a result of stress, heart rate increases, blood pressure rises, and blood flow moves away from the hands and feet, and inward toward the major organs of the body. In addition, the adrenal glands on top of the kidneys release adrenalin, stimulating the heart. Also, breathing becomes deeper and faster, while digestion slows, and perspiration increases. **(Physiology of stress)**

4. Much of what is known about the effects of stress on the body is a result of work done by the endocrinologist Hans Selye. He worked with animals in the laboratory and discovered that when the body is exposed to severe stress, it goes through a series of three stages, including alarm, resistance, and exhaustion. He referred to these stages as the General Adaptation Syndrome, or GAS. **(Physiology of stress)**

5. In the alarm stage, there is arousal of the autonomic nervous system, and the person or animal may experience shock. During the alarm stage, the resistance of the immune system also drops. With continued exposure to the stressor, the animal enters the stage of resistance, and the autonomic nervous system returns to normal, in terms of its functioning. Finally, with continued exposure to the stressor, the animal enters a phase of exhaustion. During exhaustion, the animal has difficulty adapting, resistance drops again, and the animal is prone to illness and/or death. **(Physiology of stress)**

6. Stress can be caused by catastrophic events, such as war, tornadoes, floods, and earthquakes. It can also be caused by daily annoyances, such as being stuck in traffic, having a deadline for a paper, living next door to a barking dog, and so on. Major life changes such as marriage, divorce, graduation from school, having a child, and starting a new job can also create stress. Even things thought to be desirable and positive, such as going on vacation or getting married, can cause stress. **(Causes of stress)**

7. Many of the harmful, long-term effects of stress are determined by a person's reaction to the situation or situations. Whereas Selye's model explains the biological responses to stress, it does not explain the psychological ones. Due to individual differences in temperament, personality, or emotional responsiveness, one person may find a situation to be stressful, whereas another doesn't. **(Long-term responses to stress)**

8. A very important factor that determines whether a stimulus will cause a stress reaction is the extent to which the person feels that he or she can control the situation. It has been found that rats that learn to reduce the extent of a shock by responding whenever they hear a warning tone develop fewer stomach ulcers than rats with no control. This is even the case when the rats that minimize the shock cannot completely terminate it. Therefore, even in humans, situations that allow some control or perception of control are less likely to result in stress. **(Personal control of stress)**

9. A new field of study, psychoneuroimmunology, looks at interactions between behavior and the immune system. Several researchers suggest that one's personality characteristics can affect responses to stress. In particular, it has been found that those with a Type B personality, who are more easygoing, are less likely to become ill as a result of stress. In contrast, the Type A personality, those who are competitive, impatient, and frequently exhibit negative emotions such as anger, are more susceptible to coronary disease. The Type C person, or cancer-prone person, is unassertive, patient, and holds in negative emotions such as anger. There seems to be a direct physiological connection between personality and disease. **(Immune system and stress)**

10. The immune system, the brain, and the endocrine system all interrelate in the process of dealing with stress. The immune system defends the body by destruction of foreign substances such as bacteria. It contains two types of white blood vessels referred to as lymphocytes. The immune system can overreact and attack the body's own tissue; or it can underreact, allowing cancer cells to multiply. **(Immune system and stress)**

11. Aerobic exercise that increases lung and heart fitness can help people cope with stress, lessen depression, and increase self-confidence. In numerous research studies, people in aerobic exercise programs showed such benefits compared to control groups. Aerobic exercise lowers blood pressure, and the blood pressure reaction to stress. It also increases neurotransmitters, such as serotonin, that boost mood. Other benefits include muscle relaxation, better sleep, and a sense of accomplishment. **(Relaxation)**

12. Different techniques to aid in overall relaxation include breathing deeply, meditation, deep muscle relaxation, and laughter. Research has shown that even Type A personalities can reduce their risk of heart disease by smiling, laughing, and living more leisurely. Whereas stress can increase pain, insomnia, and even decrease the capability of the immune system, meditative relaxation can counteract these effects. **(Relaxation)**

13. A connection has been discovered between social support and overall health. One explanation might be that people with strong social networks exercise more, and then eat better because their friends encourage them. Relationships can help increase self-esteem and overcome negative daily events at work or in the community. Finally, close personal relationships allow the chance to confide painful emotions to others within the network so that they don't have to be experienced alone. **(Social support)**

14. Biofeedback is a method of recording, amplifying, and giving back information about physiological activity in the body. Biofeedback research has shown that people can learn to lower their blood pressure, increase the warmth of their hands, and produce more alpha waves in the brain, which are all indicators of a relaxed state. **(Biofeedback)**

15. Cigarette smoking has been found to cause about 20 percent of all deaths in the world. Life expectancy can be increased by elimination of smoking. However, people smoke because nicotine is extremely addictive. Nicotine reaches the brain in seven seconds, arousing one to a state of alertness. Nicotine also increases heart rate and blood pressure, reduces circulation, and suppresses appetite for carbohydrates. **(Cigarette smoking)**

16. Treatments such as public health warnings, counseling, aversive conditioning, hypnosis, medical treatment, and support groups often produce results for a short period, but many resume smoking. Of people who start again, most try to quit once more. Society can do much to discourage smoking by imposing taxes, publicizing negative health effects, restricting advertising, and setting age limits on purchases. **(Cigarette smoking)**

17. Certain neurotransmitters influence emotion and behavior. For example, studies have shown that foods high in carbohydrates such as potatoes and bread increase the level of tryptophan that reach the brain. Higher levels of tryptophan raise the level of serotonin, making a person feel relaxed and less susceptible to pain. High-protein meals have been found to improve alertness and concentration. It has also been found that sugar-laden diets and high levels of fat and sodium intake can have negative effects on health. **(Diet and stress)**

18. Fat provides the body with stored energy to help when food is not available. However, today food is more available in countries like the United States, and there is little need of fat reserves. No longer is obesity adaptive. Genuine obesity increases the risk of high blood pressure, diabetes, heart disease, gall stones, and arthritis. Obesity has negative social implications as well, as there are many negative stereotypes concerning obese people. **(Diet and stress)**

19. A person should begin a diet only when self-disciplined enough to carry it through. If he or she is not disciplined, and instead engages in "yo-yo" dieting, there are increases in the risk of heart disease. This type of dieting also causes the metabolism to slow down, so that the person burns less calories at rest, making it harder to lose weight in the future. Such a diet involves a lifelong change in eating habits, paired with increased exercise. When changing one's diet, it is important to eat well-balanced meals and to keep snacking to a minimum. The reason exercise can be a benefit is that it increases one's metabolism, such that more calories are burned, even when at rest. **(Diet and stress)**

20. Research has shown that body weight is more closely related to that of one's biological parents than to an adoptive parent. Also, identical twins have similar weights, even when raised apart. However, culture also plays a role, as certain body types are reinforced by the society, depending on what is in vogue at the time. **(Diet and stress)**

Grade Yourself

Circle the numbers of the questions you missed, then fill in the total incorrect for each topic. If you answered more than three questions incorrectly, you need to focus on that topic. (If a topic has less than three questions and you had at least one wrong, we suggest you study that topic also. Read your textbook, a review book, or ask your teacher for help.)

Subject: Stress and Health

Topic	Question Numbers	Number Incorrect
Definition of stress	1, 2	
Physiology of stress	3, 4, 5	
Causes of stress	6	
Long-term responses to stress	7	
Personal control of stress	8	
Immune system and stress	9, 10	
Relaxation	11, 12	
Social support	13	
Biofeedback	14	
Cigarette smoking	15, 16	
Diet and Stress	17, 18, 19, 20	

Social Psychology

Brief Yourself

Social psychology involves the study of the effects of others on an individual. It also includes an examination of how people think about and affect, or influence one another. Social influence is powerful. It can lead people to do things as part of a group that they would not ordinarily do as an individual.

Test Yourself

1. What is suggestibility? Describe a key study conducted by Muzafer Sherif.

2. Define conformity. Mention some conditions that can strengthen conforming behavior.

3. What important work did Solomon Asch conduct on conformity?

4. What is obedience?

5. Describe the historically important research conducted by Stanley Milgram on obedience.

6. What were the main findings Milgram discovered about obedience?

7. Describe social loafing and social facilitation.

8. Define deindividuation.

9. How are group polarization and groupthink different from each other?

10. How does the Kitty Genovese murder relate to the research on bystander intervention?

11. Mention three factors involved in attraction and tell how they play a role.

12. What is passionate love?

13. Define attribution theory.

14. What is the fundamental attribution error?

15. Define cognitive dissonance.

16. How can role playing influence a person's attitudes?

17. Describe the work on role playing by Philip Zimbardo.

18. Summarize the key findings on the biology of aggression.

19. What is involved in the psychology of aggression?

20. How does television play a role in aggressive behavior?

Check Yourself

1. Suggestibility is the influence that other people have to change one's actions and opinions. For example, if someone you are talking to scratches his or her nose, you are likely to respond similarly. Sherif demonstrated how suggestibility can work by conducting a study in which he showed people a stationary dot of light in a dark room. The stationary light in the dark room creates an optical illusion, such that the dot appears to move. When Sherif asked people individually to say how much the light was moving, if at all, there were large variations in the responses. However, when the people were asked to come back two days in a row and make a judgment collectively, their estimates converged with one another, although they were never told they had to change their initial judgments. **(Suggestibility)**

2. Conformity is changing one's behavior to fit a group standard. Suggestibility is one type of conformity. Conditions that can strengthen conformity include having a group of at least three people; group status that is admired; insecure feelings on the part of the individual; no prior commitments to the group; and living in a culture that encourages respect for social norms. **(Conformity)**

3. In Asch's study, he used a problem where there was an obviously correct answer. He had four people—one subject and three confidants—judge the length of a single line to see which it matched out of group of three other lines. He found that when his confederates gave an incorrect answer before the subject responded, the rest of the group was likely to follow suit and give an obviously incorrect answer,. **(Conformity)**

4. Obedience is compliance with social pressure. It involves an outright command issued by one person to another. **(Obedience)**

5. In Milgram's classic study, he recruited a naive participant who was always the "teacher." His confederate was always the "learner." The teacher was asked to teach, and then test, pairs of words. The learner was instructed ahead of time to make certain errors. When the learner made an error, the teacher was to provide an electric shock by means of an authentic-looking control panel. In actuality, no shock was ever administered, but the teacher never realized this, as the learner acted as if he were in pain upon receiving the shock. **(Obedience)**

6. A main finding of the Milgram study on obedience was that 63 percent of the participants obeyed fully and gave the strongest electric shock, which they were told was potentially capable of killing the learner. If a teacher ever resisted, Milgram simply said something to the effect of, "You must go on." Although at the beginning of the study the teacher was told he could quit at any time and still receive his monetary compensation, the instruction to continue was sufficient to encourage the participant to obey. A lesson from this study is that ordinary people can behave in hostile and aggressive ways when instructed to obey. **(Obedience)**

7. Social loafing describes the tendency to work less hard when working as part of a group task as opposed to working independently. People in many different cultures have been shown to engage in social loafing on tasks, including tug-of-war, clapping as loud as possible while blindfolded, and shouting as loud as possible. An explanation is that people in a group feel less accountable for their actions, and therefore they rely more on other members' efforts. In contrast, social facilitation occurs when people work harder and faster in the presence of others on tasks they are good at, but perform worse on tasks they are not as good at. **(Social loafing and facilitation)**

8. Deindividuation is a circumstance in which the presence of other people is arousing, yet serves to diminish one's sense of responsibility. Deindividuation consists of becoming less self-conscious and

abandoning typical social restraints. Examples include the fact that people dressed in Ku Klux Klan hoods have been found to provide twice as much electric shock to a victim compared to those not wearing the hoods and not exercising mob behavior. **(Deindividuation)**

9. Whatever the attitudes of the members of a group are at the start of a discussion, if group members tend to favor something such as the death penalty, they will become more similar in their attitudes after group discussion. However, a group with initially dissimilar ideas will become even more dissimilar after they discuss the topic. This is referred to as group polarization. It occurs in the attitudes of individual group members. When groupthink occurs, people in the group who are in disagreement keep their ideas to themselves and, thereby, keep the group harmonious. Groupthink can lead to fiascoes, such as the Bay of Pigs invasion. In groupthink, a group tries to reach a decision, whereas group polarization can occur in any group discussing individual attitudes. **(Group effects)**

10. Kitty Genovese was murdered in 1964 in Queens, New York, outside her apartment building. The murder took place over a period of twenty minutes, yet no one came to her rescue, even though more than thirty-eight people supposedly heard her screams. This led social psychologists to examine why people who witness an emergency neglect to provide assistance. In what has been termed the "bystander effect," people are less likely to give assistance when other bystanders are present. Due to a diffusion of responsibility, there is a sense that someone else will surely help. **(Bystander effect)**

11. Three key factors in attraction are similarity, proximity, and physical appearance. People tend to like other people who are similar in levels of education, intelligence, and other attitudes and interests. There is a tendency to like those we see on a regular basis, and this is called the "mere exposure" effect. Finally, physical appearance plays a role, especially in the beginning of a relationship. People who are well dressed are more likely to make a good impression during a job interview, and people who have been independently rated as good-looking are more likely to be thought of as a desirable blind date. **(Attraction)**

12. Passionate love tends to be a temporary state. It involves physical arousal and the attempt to understand or label this arousal. Passionate love involves a release of adrenalin related to uncertainty and the fear, for example, that the object of one's affection will neglect to call again. However, once two people get to know each other better, there is more certainty and a likelihood of experiencing deeper feelings of attachment. Companionate love tends to develop later, and is involved with the development of a long-term commitment. **(Attraction)**

13. Attribution theory is the attempt to understand how a person explains another person's behaviors. Explanations for another's behavior can be based on that person's personality or on the situation that person is in. **(Attribution theory)**

14. When people commit the fundamental attribution error, they overestimate the importance of the other person's personality to explain why they are behaving in a certain way and underestimate the influence of the situation on the behavior of that person. In contract, for one's *self*, the situation is given more weight. It may be related to the focus of one's attention. The actor is focused on the situation, while observers are focused on the actor. **(Attribution theory)**

15. Cognitive dissonance refers to the tension experienced when one discovers that his or her thoughts do not match his or her actions. Cognitive dissonance can be anxiety-provoking. Awareness of cognitive dissonance often leads a person to change his or her attitudes to match his or her actions. An example is that of knowing that recycling can help save the planet's natural resources, while neglecting to recycle something such as aluminum. To reduce dissonance, the person may believe that one person can't really make a difference. **(Attribution theory)**

16. Acting out a role—such as that of taking on a new job, becoming a parent, or working as a teacher or manager—can lead the person to act the way he or she thinks a person in that role should act. At first, a person might feel odd about acting a new role, but will typically adapt, and the role becomes "real." **(Role-playing)**

17. In the 1970s, Zimbardo simulated a prison in his laboratory at Stanford University. He had college students who volunteered for the study draw straws to see who would become the prisoners, and who would become the prison guards. He gave the guards uniforms, whistles, and billy clubs, and told them to carry out certain rules. In contrast, the prisoners wore humiliating outfits and were locked in cells. Halfway into the study, the roles became so real, and the guards became so cruel and degrading, while the prisoners became more passive and experienced illness, that Zimbardo was forced to call off the study before the participants could switch roles. **(Role-playing)**

18. Aggression is verbal or physical behavior intended to hurt another. To some degree, genetics influence aggressiveness. For example, initially aggressive mice have been bred to produce even more aggressive offspring over repeated generations. Also, if one identical twin has a bad temper, the other will usually have a similar personality trait. Part of the brain called the amygdala can also lead an animal to become aggressive when stimulated. Finally, hormones and alcohol in the blood affect neural structures related to aggression. Testosterone plays a role in aggressiveness. For example, male animals become more gentle when castrated, leading to a reduction of testosterone levels. Furthermore, alcohol reduces social inhibitions against aggression. **(Aggression)**

19. People are more likely to become aggressive when frustrated. In addition, aversive events such as hot temperatures, bad smells, physical pain, and personal insults can also lead to aggressive behavior. Learning, too, plays a role. For example, children who find that their aggression successfully intimidates others may become even more aggressive in the future. Similarly, work by Bandura has shown that children who see aggressive models in person or on TV will often imitate those aggressive behaviors. Some cultures reinforce aggression and violence more than others. Aggressive behavior tendencies can be difficult to change once they have been learned. **(Aggression)**

20. Children today spend a great deal of time watching television. Every hour there are typically numerous violent acts, even during cartoons and other children's programming. Studies have shown correlations between viewing violence as a child and acting aggressively as a teenager. It is not known whether watching violence on television causes aggression. Perhaps aggressive children prefer such programming. However, there is no doubt that some relationship exists between the arousal produced by violence, the diminishing of social inhibitions against it, and imitation of what is seen on TV. **(Aggression)**

Grade Yourself

Circle the numbers of the questions you missed, then fill in the total incorrect for each topic. If you answered more than three questions incorrectly, you need to focus on that topic. (If a topic has less than three questions and you had at least one wrong, we suggest you study that topic also. Read your textbook, a review book, or ask your teacher for help.)

Subject: Social Psychology

Topic	Question Numbers	Number Incorrect
Suggestibility	1	
Conformity	2, 3	
Obedience	4, 5, 6	
Social loafing and facilitation	7	
Deindividuation	8	
Group effects	9	
Bystander effect	10	
Attraction	11, 12	
Attribution theory	13, 14, 15	
Role-playing	16, 17	
Aggression	18, 19, 20	

Also Available

Test Yourself in...

American Government

Anatomy & Physiology

Basic Math

Business Calculus

Business Law

College Chemistry

Electric Circuits

Electronic Devices and Circuits

Elementary Algebra

English Grammar

Finite Math

French Grammar

Intermediate Algebra

Introduction to Biology

Introduction to Calculus

Introduction to Data Processing

Introduction to Financial Accounting

Introduction to Managerial Accounting

Introduction to Marketing

Introduction to Psychology

Introduction to Sociology

Organic Chemistry

Physics

Precalculus Mathematics

Principles of Economics (Macroeconomics)

Principles of Economics (Microeconomics)

Spanish Grammar

Statistics

Thermodynamics

Trigonometry

. . . and many others to come!